JOURNEY
TO
SIGNIFICANCE

JOURNEY TO SIGNIFICANCE

DANIEL MCGUANE

XULON PRESS

Xulon Press
555 Winderley Pl, Suite 225
Maitland, FL 32751
407.339.4217
www.xulonpress.com

Paperback ISBN-13: 978-1-66289-140-3
Ebook ISBN-13: 978-1-66289-141-0

Acknowledgements

I want to give honor where honor is due and that is to my Lord and Savior Jesus, who has walked with me every step of my journey to significance. Significance has not come easy for me. Along the way, God has given me the privilege of meeting some very special people who have carried me when I felt insignificant. I want to thank my masters commission family for never giving up on me. I will never forget the vision God gave me of how the members of my masters commission would bring healing to me. I would also like to thank Pastor Brian for always being there for me and believing in me when I didn't believe in myself. Pastor Keith, who was my first father figure, who told me he loved me, and I knew he meant it. I also want to thank Jennifer, she has been an encouragement and has been there for me. Through you guys, I have learned to speak life, through you guys, A big Thank you from me to Dr Audrey who has walked with me in this journey for over 10 years in helping me recover from grief, childhood trauma and more importantly has been a consistant mom to me over the years speaking life and hope over me . I have learned to believe in myself. Through you guys, I've learned to dream.

Table of Contents

Preface

The idea for *Journey to Significance* came to me one day as I was looking at a picture that overlooked a city with a fence in front of the city. The image was an arial view of a city surrounded by a gate intended to keep harm away from the residents within. Yet the gate's very presence revealed the residents' fear, and fear paralyzes... When I saw that image I realized the vast beauty that this cityscape has and how it could give us a glimpse into the vast love that God has for us and wants to reveal to us. I thought, *How many times do we paralyze ourselves every day by limiting ourselves in what we can do?* That's what the fence represents and shows that obstacles like this can paralyze us and cause us to be stuck behind something our whole life. Has there ever been a time in your life that you felt stuck in wondering if you are significant? This journey is very personal for me because I've allowed myself to be paralyzed because of fear and insecurities. I would compare myself to others and wish I had what they had, not recognizing the countless blessings God has gifted me with. I am learning, however, that significance begins with the inner appearance of someone, not their outward appearance. Maybe, like myself, someone reading this book has been wounded by words of others, and those words have caused them to be crippled and left feeling insignificant.

If so, remember this: Insignificance is a byproduct of the devil. Any time you feel insignificant, remember that the feeling is only a great reminder of how significant you truly are in God's eyes. It's time we as the children of the King of Kings and lose the chains of insignificance the devil has placed on us. It's time we rise up in the power of Christ and call ourselves blessed, even when no one else says we're blessed. Rise up and speak life.

Introduction

Significance is born over time; the more we see who God created us to be the more we can see how truly significant we are as His children. Significance is not an outward view; You are worthy of attention, You are important in the eyes of God, the inward view from the perspective of a loving Father! Becoming significant is more than a day long process It's a building process, it's becoming the significant you that God has called you to be Jeremiah 29:11 NIV. Significance is not a decision. It's not waking up one day and deciding, "I am significant," and significance simply occurs. Do not get me wrong, we all have significance within each of us; however, we should continue to develop our significance. recognizing that they are worth it even though others may not see that.

Your significance as a person is not in how based on much you do, how much you know, or even how talented you are. Being a person of significance begins and ends with your identity in Christ. Throughout this book I hope to empower, inspire, and encourage each reader as they undertake their own journey to significance.To be of significance" Means to matter, count, signify, be of importance, be relevant, make a difference. Significance should first and foremost reflect what God says you are You are God's Son, you God's Daughter, The Greatest reference of Value that we have is found in Christ. Any perspective outside of that could produce a mixed view of what our significance truly is and where it comes from.

Anything that you do in life can be significant. Imagine with me for a moment that we could change our culture and society by rising and becoming people of significance in life.

1

From Insignificance to Significance

*For I know the plans I have for you," Declares the Lord,
"Plans to prosper you and not to harm you, plans to give
you a hope and a future.*
—Jeremiah 29:11 NIV

How we view ourselves on the inside often reveals how we view ourselves on the outside. From early childhood to being a young adult I struggled with feeling so insignificant, as if I had nothing to offer, while everyone else had something to give. From the age of ten to the age of twenty-one I felt that way because of disabilities that I have had, because of not being able to fit in, with being completely deaf in my left ear, with having a stuttering problem. I have often wondered what makes someone significant and how a person becomes significant today. Now, I know that the way you see yourself today is the way you will see yourself tomorrow, and the day after tomorrow, so the answer to significance must be, in part, how a person sees himself or herself.

The Bible says that we are created in the image of God (Gen. 1:27 NIV). Right there is a truth that should encourage you and cause you to recognize that you are significant. But before insignificance can be turned into success stories, into significance, is necessary to learn from past failures and past mistakes. Often, the reason people feel insignificant is because of past failures and mistakes. To overcome those mistakes and failures we must allow them to become our greatest teachers, teachers that propel us to move from insignificance to significance.

Significance Today

The world celebrates significance and the thoughtless words of others directed toward someone can be the greatest weapons of insignificance. Many people feel insignificant today. What if you look at yourself daily in the mirror and say "I am significant in the eyes of God! I am a beloved Son and Daughter of God, and no one can take that away from."

What achievements, personal characteristics, or possessions in our culture and society today appear in your mind when you think of people today who have influence?

Well, guess what? The exact same people who began to appear in your mind that are significant many have also felt insignificant at one point or another in their lives, and if they can become significant, you can too!

Stolen Significance

The thief comes only to steal and kill and destroy; I have come that they may have life, and have it to the full.
—John 10:10 NIV

If someone's significance is stolen, their values, self-esteem, worth, and confidence are stolen. one of the greatest ways to get your significance back is to change the way you view yourself as an individual. Significance begins within a person; significance is not determined by someone's background or heritage, or what others say about them.

If you have lost your significance, it's time for you take back what is rightfully yours. Here are five reasons why it's time to take it back.

1 **God doesn't make junk**. The Bible says that you were created in God's image, which means your significance is found in Genesis 1, "Then God said let us make man in our own Image, according to our likeness" (Gen. 1:26 NIV). Your significance is in and through Him alone!

2 **God will do what you can't; stop making excuses**. In Exodus 4 Moses said to the Lord, "O Lord, I

have never been eloquent, neither in the past nor since you have spoken to your servant. I am slow of speech and tongue" (Ex. 4:10 NIV). I encourage reading the remaining verses in chapter 4. Nothing is impossible for God to do through you. Just watch God at His best working in and through us when we give Him our little bit.

3   **It's never too late.** Young or old, it's never too late to regain your significance back for His purposes. With significance also comes wisdom; it's never too late to gain wisdom from those who have gone ahead of us. Just as it is valuable for young people to regain their significance, it is also important for the older generations to regain their significance. Some of the most significant people in our society, both young and old, are trapped in insignificance.

4   **Your beginning is not you're ending.** God can't fail, Its not his nature to fail us. The Bible tells us, Being Confident of this, that he who began a good work in you will carry it on to completion until the day of Christ Jesus" (Phil. 1:6 NIV). Again, your beginning is not you're ending. How many have started out on the journey of significance and lost sight of our real meaning and purpose Have you ever felt like I have tried to be a person of significance. Can I encourage you to

have a one-day-at-a-time approach? Instead of having the thoughts that say, *What's wrong with me?* believe that you can, and then you can begin to say, *What is right with me? What am I doing, even if it's the smallest of things, to become a person who pursues significance to the best of my abilities!*

5 **Rise up! Rise above the circumstance.** We've got one of two choices, we can either choose to rise and take back our significance in the name of Jesus, or we can continue to be crippled in our minds, and hearts, which leads to being insignificant. For the next month, watch the words that come out of your mouth. Your words will reveal "your words reveal your thought process, your beliefs. Your thoughts eventually form your actions.". The circumstances should never be a factor in our significance. The difficulties in our journeys reveal how truly significant we are for his kingdom. Scripture warns us, "Be alert and of sober mind. Your enemy the devil prowls around like a roaring lion looking for someone to devour" (1 Peter 5:8 NIV). Feeling insignificant paralyzes heart, mind, body, and soul. In contrast, believing in your significance produces action.

6 **Find your significance in who you are.** Does the Bible tell us how to find our significance? As we

dissect each of these questions, I believe each of us falls into one of these three categories. We are either on a journey to significance, and we are learning what makes someone significant; or we are trying to figure out what the Bible says about significance.

How do you become significant? Becoming significant is no easy task; it takes hard work. Psalm 37 tells us to, "Take delight in the LORD, and he will give you the desires of your heart. / Commit your way to the LORD; trust in him and he will do this" (Psalm 37:4–5 NIV). Anyone who is significant will always tell you that they are committed to what they do; you can't become significant at something unless you're committed to something. God was committed to us. People who are significant are always committed to the small things first.

Shift from insignificance to significance.

One of the steps to becoming a person of significance is recognizing that there will be times of failure, but we must never allow times of quitting. It is important to renew your mind daily in your journey to significance. Renewing your mind allows you to stay focused on the journey. The Bible instructs us to, Do not conform to the patterns of the world, but be transformed by the renewing of your mind. Then you will be to test and approve what

God's will is - His good, pleasing and perfect will" (Rom. 12:2 NIV).

To become a person of significance, you must first become disciplined in your heart, mind, and soul. I believe one of the main reasons so many people feel insignificant today is because of the battle that is going on in their minds. The more you think something, the more you become that thing. To grow our significance, we must have our minds renewed.

Thoughts of insignificance must cease to control us. Could it be that the reason so many people feel insignificant. To grow in significance, you must not allow your thoughts to control you. Instead, you must control your thoughts; you must think thoughts that move you toward significance.

I have often wondered about these questions. I know Romans 12:2 tells us to "be transformed by the renewing of your mind," but I've often wondered what practical steps we can take to renew our minds. How can we recognize a specific thought pattern that decreases our significance in Christ? Is the battle of significance won in our minds or in our hearts? Does the environment you grew up in determine how to review yourself and how you see yourself?

I want to take you on a journey to discover biblical answers to these four questions. I also want to share some practical ways to control our thoughts which will help us renew our minds.

How can we control our thoughts?

First, consider our thoughts about others. Thoughts of self, Every day we are confronted with the reality of our thoughts, thoughts that no one else knows except for us. No one else can control our thoughts except for us. It's not enough for us to learn to uplift others; we must learn how to quiet the negative behavior in our thought patterns. We can't speak well about someone, yet in our thoughts be condemning them.Negative internal thoughts can often times disrupt how we view ourselves, and ultimately blur the vision of who God says we are. That's why it's so important that we learn how to control our thoughts. When you have thoughts toward others and yourself, does feel like it's helping you, or is it creating a more a downward spiral?

What are some motives that have led us to thinking the way that we think, and how can we control those motives in our thought process? I grew up in a negative environment where I was constantly put down which led to years of feeling unqualified and insignificant. Being told I was never enough or good enough began to make believe that was true for so many years. A motive always begins with a thought, As the thought develops, it gives birth to a motive, a reason to do or say something. A motive, like our thoughts, often reveals our character. The fear of failure, rejection, loss are just a few motives that have led so many to let their thoughts run rampant.

Take a couple of moments daily to ground your thoughts. Take a deep breath and allow yourself to give space and grace to every thought that brings you down, controlling your thoughts allows you to create a new pathway. It gives you the perspective to ask, If a thought comes and says, *I am not good enough,* why not exhale that feeling and calmly say to yourself, *I am good enough?*

Finally, Brothers, whatever is true, whatever is noble, whatever is right, whatever is pure, whatever is lovely, whatever is admirable—if anything is excellent or praise-worthy—think about such things.
(Philippians 4:8 NIV)

We can find some practical ways to control our thoughts in this verse. I think we all fall into the trap of negativity at one point or another. To overcome these thoughts, we must constantly train our minds to discern what is right and eliminate what is wrong. We must confront the wrong thought by denying its claim and reclaiming the verse above. We constantly cast stones at ourselves through our thoughts.

We must train our minds to forget all the wrongs of the past, and to instead remember all the rights done by us and to us. We can't change yesterday's insignificance, but we can change today and become significant. Refuse to linger on past mistakes. Paul, the writer of the Romans, chose to forget those things that were behind and look ahead to the future.

There is this saying that says, "get your mind out of the gutter," when our minds dwell on impure thoughts. Some readers might wonder what this has to do with significance. Anybody who harbors impure thoughts about themselves in their minds will likely feel impure about themselves on the outside to. They betray themselves by doing stuff they that said they would never do, by being controlled by thoughts of feeling no good, by being controlled by thoughts of being worthless, by being controlled by thoughts of guilt, shame, sorrow. That thinking steals our significance. I have been there before, controlled by a negative mindset toward myself and others.

To eliminate the problem, instead of focusing on negative feelings, think about the good things in yourself and in people. Think about how blessed you are. Think about what you can do. not what you can't do.

Have you ever been around someone who is always positive? Someone who always has this determination that they can accomplish anything if they put their mind to it? I believe it's because they have learned to praise themselves, not in a prideful way, but in a way that speaks life into themselves and those around them. Those who speak life never seem to get down on themselves by allowing negative thoughts to override their thoughts of accomplishing something now. See, you can build yourself up in significance by speaking life over where you are now, and accomplish something where you are in life now, not where you want to be in the future. Doing this prepares you for the next step in your journey to significance and continued diligence in self-monitoring negative or harmful thoughts combined with revising them into life-giving thoughts will guide you toward your larger, later goals.

One of greatest weapons the devil will use (and he will use anything against us) are thoughts of self-hatred. He would love to have us use our thoughts to condemn ourselves in our own minds. If he can control you through your thoughts, causing self-hatred, then he can control your significance. Think about whatever is lovely. You were created in the image of God. We must learn how to love ourselves for who we are, for who God has created us to be in his kingdom. We must kill the giant of negative, hurtful, even sinful, thought patterns instead of feeding the thought patterns that have harmed us. God has given us his word ingrained in Scripture, so that his Word can become ingrained in our thoughts and in our minds. We think, reflect, dwell, and meditate daily on Philippians 4:8.

Let this Mind be in you as it was also in Christ Jesus.
(Philippians 2:5 NIV)

Recognize and Eliminate Your Own Significance Decreasing Thought Patterns to Increase Significance in Christ

Thought patterns that decrease our significance in Christ are not developed overnight. They develop over time through the seeds that we allow to be planted into our minds through entertainment we choose, through those we hang around with, and through how we perceive ourselves. We're allowing negative or harmful thought seeds to be planted into our minds, and as the seeds grow, they produce that thought pattern.

To recognize a specific thought pattern about feeling insignificant, we must first discover where that thought was first developed. I know for me it was developed through the words of others. While growing up I heard words like "You're worthless," and as I dwelled on that thought of feeling worthless, I birthed that thought pattern. To increase significance, it is necessary to rediscover the way your thought patterns are cycled. It is necessary to find what triggers the destructive thought patterns, what events, words, or thoughts bring back memories of feeling insignificant. Finding the trigger points of what makes us feel insignificant is necessary so we can edit these negative thoughts, these lies, into truths.

How often do we truly take the time to think about what thought patterns we are allowing into our minds? I have come to realize that no one but you can cause you to be insignificant. When we think we are insignificant, we are insignificant. In contrast, once we begin to think we are significant, we begin to believe we are significant. Let's explore some areas where thought patterns of insignificance are developed.

I think we need someone else to help us correct our thoughts"...or "we need someone else to say or act differently, so we can change our thoughts." Maybe even write "we blame others for our thoughts," meaning, we justify our thoughts, because they are based on the words and actions of others. or we play the blame game and make excuses for how we've developed harmful thought patterns that contribute to our feelings of insignificance. It is our responsibility to train our minds to begin to reverse our thinking, to reverse negative or sinful thought by replacing it with a positive or God-confirming thought. Consider the following examples.

When the thought of being a failure comes to mind, what is usually the first thing we are trained to do? For me, at least, I usually dwell on the thought and become that thought. To reverse the thought, I begin to speak, "I am winner. I can make a difference. I can overcome this. I am child of the King." It is critical that you stop convincing yourself that you can't stop your negative and harmful thoughts.

Our potential is locked up within us when we think that what we have won't ever make a difference and we allow our minds to become undisciplined. This occurs when we dwell on what we can't do instead of what we can do. Instead of thinking about what we can't do, let's begin to think about what we can do and allow those thoughts to cause us to rise again in our significance in Christ.

Allowing the wrong voices to control your thoughts is detrimental to your significance. The saying, "Who we are around is who will become" is so true. It's more than likely that the thought patterns of the people you are around will become your own.

Is the Battle Won in Hearts or Minds?

I believe the battle is won in both our hearts and minds. We can't master our thoughts inside our minds without first disciplining our hearts with our thoughts. Neither can we master our hearts without first disciplining the thoughts of our minds.

The Mind Battle

The mind is the seat of thought and memory; it is the center of consciousness that generates thoughts, feelings, ideas, and perceptions, and it stores knowledge and memories. It is so easy to deceive ourselves to think something that's not true. For many of us, our minds deceive us each day with thoughts of feeling no good, with thoughts of feeling insignificant, with thoughts of failures. Every thought remains in the seat of consciousness.

We must learn how to refocus the lens of our mind on what is lovely, what is right, what is noble, what is pure, and what is praiseworthy. If we learn how to refocus our thoughts toward positive thoughts, we will journey from insignificance to significance. The Bible says, "'For my thoughts are not your thoughts, neither are your ways my ways,' declares the Lord. 'As the heavens are higher than the earth, so are my ways higher than your ways and my thoughts than your thoughts'" (Isa. 55:8–9 NIV).

We must break the cycle of conforming to our old thought patterns and instead be transformed by new thought patterns created by the renewing of our minds in the kingdom Do not conform to the pattern of this world, But be transformed by the renewing of your mind. Then you will be able to test and approve what God's will is-his good, pleasing and perfect will. (Romans 12:2 NIV).

Psychological Warfare

The battle begins in the mind. Many people beat themselves up psychologically every day, and they have lost their significance. They have lost the will to fight. To avoid this trap of the devil, we need to relearn how to think. We must learn how to re-maneuver our minds to shift from one mindset to a better mindset. We must learn how to manipulate our minds into thought patterns that will create a positive outlook on life no matter what the circumstance might be.

Our thoughts, our feelings, are manifested outwardly, so we must redirect our own minds from thoughts of insignificance to thoughts of our significance in Christ.

Heart Basis of Emotional Life: The heart is the metaphoric source and center of emotional life, where the deepest and sincerest feelings are located, and where each person is most vulnerable to pain.

Our heart is the center piece of our soul, the battle for significance always begins in our minds, but the battle for significance always ends in our hearts. The heart of a person shows their desire to succeed. The heart of a person shows who they truly are. Their hearts reflect how much they believe in themselves. To feel insignificant, we have to learn to encourage ourselves in the Lord as Psalm 42 tells us: "Why, my soul, are you downcast? Why so disturbed within me? Put your hope in God, for I will yet praise Him, my Savior, and my God" (Psalm 42:5 NIV).

Truth

To find our significance, we first must discover the truth about ourselves. Truth is knowing what is between the lines, knowing what is right and wrong. Significance has been lost due to the current identity crisis of humanity. Everybody is trying to be somebody else instead of being true to themselves. Often, to find out the truth about something, we must see the whole picture of the individual.

Seeing the whole picture enables us to find the root issue of why we feel insignificant.

Significance is often rooted in issues that we chase after, love on, believe in, and deal with to grow from insignificance to becoming a person of significance. Hosea 4:6 NIV my people are destroyed from lack of knowledge. " Because you have rejected knowledge, I also reject you as my priests; because you have ignored the law of God, I also will ignore your children. People perish every single day because they don't have the knowledge (the truth) about themselves. Jesus answered "I am the way the Truth and the life. No one comes to the father except through me" (John 14:6 NIV). Truth is only found in God. When we find truth in God, we can find truth in ourselves in our journey to significance.

Five Behaviors That Decrease Significance

1. Trying to be somebody that they're not. "Either significance will be created by an individual who refuses to conform to society's lies and instead be renewed by God's Word (Jesus) or insignificance will occur because an individual feels left out or left behind by popular culture if they trade their God-given identity and peace for a fabrication of the world." Significance will either be driven by someone, or significance will drive someone..

2. Words hurt and words wound, and words can leave people crippled for the rest of their lives. The words of others left me wounded for a long time. The words of others have left me paralyzed, unable to believe in myself. Their words have left me broken, feeling like that there were no hope for me. More than likely, some of you who are reading this are probably reminded of words spoken over them by others. Know this: The words of others wouldn't define us if we knew the truth about ourselves. The words of other's wouldn't break us if we set our hearts on the truth of who our identity was truly found in—Jesus.

3. Becoming comfortable. It's so easy to become comfortable in something and become complacent. Being significant requires the person to be uncomfortable at times. Those who are comfortable are usually those who wait for something to happen instead of making something happen. Being a person of significance is no easy task, it's not going to be a walk in the park, and it's not going to happen in our timing but in God's perfect timing—his timing is always the correct timing for our lives even when we don't understand it.

4. Becoming complacent self-satisfied, smug, content, self-righteous, and disapproving can also

cause feelings of insignificance. When someone becomes satisfied in what they have and have given up on pursuing new things, after a while they begin to experience feelings of insignificance. What they were first known for has been forgotten about, and that has caused them to feel insignificant. I believe there are people who live their lives in complacency who could become highly significant because of their God-given talents; however, unused, their gifts begin to diminish. The greatest mistake we can make is to allow ourselves to become complacent and content and thus allow ourselves to be stopped in our journey without even realizing it.

5. Being paralyzed by buying into the belief that you are insignificant. Let me paint you a picture. There is a wheelchair in the middle of the room, the wheelchair represents us. How many times do we place ourselves in that wheelchair by giving ourselves excuses, telling ourselves we can't do it, we can't make it, and/or we will fail at it. Every time we speak against ourselves in such a way, we give permission to our very own words to paralyze us. No matter what has had you paralyzed, you can rise up and begin again on your journey to significance. God values you more than you value you.

God values your significance more than you value it yourself.

Rise up. Rise above the mundane. Rise up out of the old garments, the garments of feeling insignificant.

Insignificance begins as a seed, but we give birth to that seed by how we nurture it. Do we nurture significant or insignificant seeds? What we nurture will reveal itself through our thoughts, feelings, and actions. As for me, I have cultivated a lot of birth defects in insignificance, and I had to realize that it's up to me up to fix the defects. How I view myself is revealed, too, in how I speak about myself and in how I believe in myself, and, most importantly, in how I see myself. The only way I can see my true self, and go from insignificance to significance, is to capture the father's heart and see how he views me.

Let us declare that, in Jesus's name, we will no longer view ourselves as insignificant. We cast down the thought patterns that cause us to view ourselves in a way that steals away our God-given significance. Instead, we declare, "Therefore, if anyone is in Christ Jesus, he is a new creation in Jesus. The old is gone and the new has come" (2 Cor. 5:17 NIV).

Let's Pray:

Father, we recognize that you gifted us with life; that you are the giver of life. Lord, thank you for making all things new. Lord Jesus, help us to no longer live in our old ways. We cast down our old ways, and instead we put on the new ways of you, Lord Jesus, help us to live significant lives for the purposes of the kingdom and help us to find our significance in you. In Jesus's name. Amen.

2

Be the True You;
Be True to Yourself

*For you created my inner most being you
knit me together in my mother's womb.*
—Psalm 139:13 NIV

The scripture that begins this chapter is one of my life verses. Have you ever thought to yourself, *Do I have what it takes to succeed in life? Do I have what it takes to be a man or woman of God?*

I believe we have lost the perspective to see ourselves as we are created, and our perspective of ourselves has become distorted. I've struggled with the questions above all my life; I still struggle with them to this day. If you have struggled with these questions too, help to answer them follows.

Seek God to Find the Answers

Throughout this chapter, we'll look at each of these questions. We will approach them from a standpoint of how you feel about these questions, and we will also discover what God has to say about these questions. One of the reasons I've struggled with these questions is because of the walls that have been up in my life.

We must open the door of our hearts to him from the inside because the doorknob to our heart is on the inside of our heart.[1] In order to have these questions answered, we should learn how to ask the right questions at the right time, and we have to seek God.

You will seek me and find me when you have seek me
with all of your heart.
—Jeremiah 29:13 NIV

The key to being true to yourself and being the true you is to find the true you; the key is to discover who God says you are. Stop trying to please everybody else; stop being somebody that you're not in front of others.. People care how well you carry yourself by just being yourself; by being yourself you free yourself to just be you. It takes more work to be someone you're not than just being yourself. The thing about being somebody that you're not is that people can tell that you're faking it. People can also tell when you're just being you.

When you go into an interview, apply for something, ask for a loan, or anything like that, what is the first thing people will recommend that you do? They always tell you to just be yourself; don't pretend to be somebody else.

Could it be that the reason why so many people are not true to themselves by being their true selves is because they don't like themselves? We must change the misconception that has been planted and birthed in the heart of humanity? What if we could change this misconception and turn it into conception? Misconception of yourself can cause birth defects; true conception of yourself reassures you that you can be you.

Only You Can Take Away You

Your greatest advantage in every situation is to just be yourself. Your greatest disadvantage in every situation is to try to be someone that you're not. You have advantages to being true to yourself. There's only one you. If God wanted there to be another you, he would've created another you.

Just as there are advantages to being yourself, there are disadvantages to trying to be somebody that you're not. First, pretending to be someone you're not takes away everything that God has placed inside you. When people are trying to be somebody else, they're posing, trying to be like somebody they truly not. When you are yourself, you win. When you are trying to be somebody that you're not, you lose. Your responsibility is to be you. Remember the old saying, "Be yourself?" It's not your responsibility to try to be someone you're not.

One of the greatest tragedies that happens to individuals is the tragedy of losing oneself and instead become another self. The definition of tragedy is: "A serious play with a tragic theme, often involving a heroic struggle and the downfall of the main character. Stay true to who God says you are. Stay true to what you know your gifts are. Stay true to who your friends say you are. If, we lose that, we lose everything. Your character is developed daily by being yourself. And, yes, there will be obstacles and hurdles to overcome, but the only way to overcome them is by being yourself.

Your character can be your greatest asset to your journey to significance. Synonyms of character include the following: asset, strength, benefit, plus (informal), plus point, positive feature, quality, skill, talent, ability, qualification, power, endowment, boon, blessing, resource. With, your character is essential to your journey to significance. Each one of those qualities that you read are given to you as an individual. Each of those assets only comes through hard work and discipline and the desire to become significant. No one can make you significant except you, which requires the internal desire to become significant by being yourself.

Now, let's answer the questions we asked at the start of this chapter.

Do I Have What It Takes?

All of us have asked that question. If there is breath left in your body, you have what it takes to be you. Anybody who lives a significant life can tell you that they didn't achieve their significance by trying to be somebody they're not. They achieved it by being themselves. People need people like you to be you. People don't need you to act like someone that you're not.

Truthfully, people pleasing will get you nowhere. God pleasing will get you anywhere he has designed you to be. Scripture says, "Take delight in the Lord, and he will give you the desires of your heart. 5 Commit your way to the Lord; trust in him and he will do this" (Psalm 37:4–5 NIV). These verses are so important to seizing your full potential and seeing that you do have what it takes.

Before you question whether you have what it takes, do exactly what Psalm 37 says to do. The best way to find out what we are good at doing is by asking the father what he has created us to be good at doing. Check out what Jesus says in But seek first his kingdom and his righteousness, and all these things will be given to you as well" (Matt. 6:33 NIV). Everything that Jesus says is true. We must seek first his kingdom instead of seeking first what we want to succeed in. When we seek to do things on of our own will to succeed, we fail at succeeding. In contrast, when we seek to succeed in what he has called us to succeed in we will succeed.

The question is not if people say you have what it takes or if you think you have what it takes, the question turns on what God has to say. You have what it takes to do what he's gifted you with, but you don't have what it takes to do what you're not gifted in doing.

We are good at giving ourselves a false sense of identity, and these self-created false selves strip away our identity.

We must let go of this false sense of insecurity we get by trying to be everybody else, and not being ourselves in everyday life. The reason so many people lose their significance is by trying to be somebody they lose their sense of security within themselves to accomplish what only they can accomplish. But they can't accomplish it without first learning how to be themselves in front of other people.

Your primary focus should not be on whether you have what it takes to accomplish the things Good has given to you. Your primary focus needs to be on whether you believe in yourself and can see those things accomplished. First, to see if you truly have what it takes, you must look inside your heart. Everybody has what it takes to accomplish something, but not everybody accomplishes something. Everybody can expand in their significance, but not everybody chooses to expand in their significance.

When you read the question, "Do you have what it takes?" what's the first question that pops into your mind? The only way you will ever see if you have what it takes is to launch out into the places that are comfortable for you to expand your talents.

Do I Have What It Takes to Succeed in Life?

As we go through this second question, let's look at some scriptures in Philippians that speak to what God has to say about you succeeding in life, being confident of this, that he who began a good work in you will carry it on to completion until the day of Christ Jesus (Philippians 1:6 NIV) God began a good work in you. He began the work of Jesus through you that carries out the good work in you using the talents he has entrusted you with, which flow out of you for you to succeed in life. God wants you to succeed, the heart of Abba Father leaps when his children succeed.

The greatest way for you to succeed is by stepping out of the old garments of insignificance into the arms of Jesus, into your significance. The definition for "succeed" is this. "Make significant progress to do well in an activity, making admirable progress or recording impressive achievements."[2] Life is too short for you not to succeed. Succeed by doing what you can do. Don't waste time trying to do what you can't do.

To realizes your full potential, you must attain something in order to gain something. Nothing can be gained without first attaining something. To attain something is no easy task. It takes hard work, discipline, and a desire to persevere when you want to give up.

Have you met someone who won't give up no matter what, someone who refuses to quit? Even when everyone else says they can't do it, they still have the resolve within themselves to succeed. I believe one of the reasons that they succeed is because they surround themselves with people who influence them in ways that help them become significant. People influence people. Think of someone who has had a significant impact on your life. Whoever you are around will influence you, so succeeding in significance requires you to pursue relationships with people who influence significance in you.

Your level of confidence that you do have what it takes to succeed is important, because your level of determination to succeed determines how far you succeed. When you are determined to succeed, you discover these characteristics: strength of mind, willpower, resolve, purpose, fortitude, and grit to succeed. People who live significant lives constantly challenge themselves to expand, to grow, their success.

Surround yourself with people who will challenge you to succeed in everyday life, people who will challenge you in ways that will make you grow. By doing this, you will realize that you can succeed, that you do have what it takes to succeed. Then, when you succeed, you can help other people realize that they can succeed too.

One of the greatest ways to succeed is to never give up. Winston Churchill said, "Never Give Up. Never, Never, Never Give up."[3] Too many people never succeed because they give up on themselves before they can ever give themselves a chance to succeed. Remember, too, that succeeding is more than a daily activity; it's a daily lifestyle, a daily commitment, and a daily discipline. To succeed, you must train yourself to succeed in your chosen place or activity.

The Definition of *Lifestyle*: "Manner of living, the way of life characteristic of a particular person, group or culture."[4] Lifestyles are cultivated every day. A lifestyle for someone can be how they view life, how they view themselves, how they view various values. Lifestyles begin to develop in us when we are children and carry onward into our adult lives. It is possible to change a lifestyle because lifestyles don't adapt to us we adapt to the lifestyle, The standard in which you live is based on the standard of how you discipline your lifestyle.

Daily Lifestyle My question is this: Are you enabling yourself to succeed? If what you are succeeding at doesn't cause you to stretch yourself, then maybe it's time to stretch yourself further into a lifestyle of succeeding.

Often, we fall so short of reaching the success finish line that we begin to believe we will never make anything out of our lives. If you have ever believed, thought, or adopted that statement into your life, you should know it's a lie from the pits of hell. The devil would like nothing more than to stop you from succeeding.

A person who succeeds is someone who enquires of himself and of God how to make success a daily lifestyle. It has been said that King David acquired himself to the Lord, which means that, before he did anything he first made sure with God that it was something he would succeed in.

When you breath your last breath, would people follow your lifestyle because you lived a life of significance? What you're remembered by often reveals the lifestyle you held.

Daily Commitment

What is your commitment? If you can answer those questions, then you can find out what you will succeed in. We can be committed to something for all the wrong reasons. Commitment is not revealed by how much you do; commitment is revealed by how much you have grown when the difficult times come. Those who have made a positive difference today are those who stayed the course and remained committed. Marriages would last if we would stay committed. The apostle Paul talks about staying the course. Could it be that, if we stay committed, people could be restored and see who they are in Christ? Commitment goes far beyond what we perceive it to be. The cry of my heart is to make a positive difference in the heart of humanity by making a significant difference, which means that, no matter the cost, I will stay committed to the cause.

What could cause you to break your commitment to becoming significant? It's easy to stay committed when everyone else is committed, but your commitment speaks more loudly when you're committed when no one else is committed. If we can't stay committed to things God has placed before us, then we will never be able to stay committed to the things he has for us later. If God can't trust us now to be committed, how can he trust us to be committed later? Respect is earned through the commitment of others. I don't know about you, but for me it's easy to stay committed to the big things. It's the small things where I find myself uncommitted a lot of times. But it's our commitment to the small things that causes us to be committed to the big things.

Daily Discipline

The first step to being significant is to live a disciplined daily lifestyle. I have always thought that anybody who makes a difference, anyone who has significant influence, never had to work for it—that they never had to pay a price for it. Man was I wrong! Being a person of significance has a price tag on it, anything that anybody does that has to do with making a difference in the others always comes with a cost.

A disciplined daily lifestyle will challenge you. Being disciplined means doing something that you don't want to do but doing it out of a motivation to accomplish something. Let's bring some simplicity to this. College students always have to study and put in long hours daily in order to earn the degrees that they are seeking. The same is true with anyone pursuing significance. Significance is always determined by the discipline of a person. When pursuing significance, everything else will eventually fail if the person is not leading a disciplined lifestyle.

I believe one of the main reasons King David was called a man after God's own heart in First Samuel 13:14 was because he had these three qualities: first, he had the will to succeed; second, he had a daily commitment to succeed; and third, he had the daily discipline required to succeed. Now, the question is this: How do we put into practice these three disciplines? Let's look at each of these disciplines. David was a man who knew God from the inside out, and of course God knew him from the inside out. The more you get to know God, the more you get to know yourself

The Definition of Daily Discipline: "Calm controlled behavior: The ability to behave in a controlled and calm way even in a difficult or stressful situation." There is a saying, "the little foxes spoil the vine." I can handle big situations, but it's those little issues in life where I find myself with lack of discipline. One of the most dangerous acts you can do in lacking discipline is to become prideful in realizing that you have what it takes. Scripture warns us, "Pride goes before destruction, a haughty spirit before a fall" (Prov. 16:18 NIV). The only way to keep from becoming prideful is by living a disciplined lifestyle that causes you to become humble. The second definition for daily discipline is, "Conscious control over a lifestyle: Mental self-control used in directing or changing behavior, learning something, or training for something." One of the greatest ways to succeed and become significant is to stay underneath the umbrella of humility. When someone becomes so used to succeeding and being significant, it can be so easy to begin to exalt him- or herself instead of exalting the one who truly deserves the honor, Father God.

When significant lives are lived out every single day, we must make sure that we are in accordance with these three scriptures:

> God opposes those with pride but gives grace to the humble. (James 4:6 NIV)

> Humble yourselves therefore, under God's mighty hand, that he may lift you up in due time. (1 Peter 5:6 NIV)

> He who dwells in the shelter of the highest will rest under the shadow of the almighty. I will say of the Lord he is my refuge, and my fortress, my God in whom I will trust. (Psalm 91:1–2 NIV)

When Succeeding, Stay Away from These Three Traps

Trap 1: Pride

Pride is when you allow yourself to be exalted. Pride traps many of us. God specifically says in his word what pride will do to someone. Did you know the devil was kicked out of heaven because of pride? Pride was the first sin. If you're going to boast about anything, boast about the significance that the Lord has given you to influence others. If you want to continue in your journey to significance, you must kill pride, which is the exact opposite of humility.

Trap 2: Living a Selfish Life

A selfish person only looks out for what is best for him or her. A selfish person only wants things done that can benefit them. A selfish mentality is one that asks, What benefit will I get out of it? Significance is putting others before yourself. Said another way, it's wanting others to be preferred to you. Do we constantly put ourselves before others, or do we put others before ourselves? A selfish person looks after his or her desire only. For me, it's sometimes easy to ignore the needs of others, but I don't want to ever ignore my own needs. We live in a society of self-centered people that are self-seeking, self-interested, and self-regarding.

Trap 3: Relying on Your Own Strength and Abilities to Succeed

If what you build is not built through the strength and abilities that God has given you, then the foundation of your success will only last for a season. If you look at society through the eyes of those who are succeeding, what they have built will crumble if it's not built on the sold rock of Christ succeeding in the eyes. We live in stubborn and prideful society that says we can do it ourselves; that we don't need any help. How many of us have said that the reason we want to do things without any help is because of pride?

Three Success Launch Pads

Launch Pad 1: Stay Humble

Humility is always the number one factor in succeeding. People are not drawn to cocky people; people are drawn to those who live a life of humility. Staying humble enables you to remain under God's umbrella of succeeding. Sure, if you are not under his umbrella, you will still succeed, but ask yourself this question:

There is something different about people who walk in humility. They attract people to themselves. God promises to protect the humble in scripture, "The Lord sustains the humble but casts the wicked to the ground. (Psalm

147:6 NIV). Humility can also mean that you put others before your own self. If we could learn that principle—putting others before ourselves—then we can learn what it truly means to succeed. When you walk in humility, you will not have to fight to succeed. No, success will just come to you. The Bible says, Humble yourselves, therefore, under God's mighty hand, that he may he will lift you up in due time" (1 Peter 5:6 NIV). The thing about succeeding that we must realize and understand is that, as long as we continue to do what God says to do, when he says to do it, he will lift us up in due time.

Launch Pad 2: Honoring God in Everything We Do: If we honor God, God will honor us. Honoring God means bringing recognition to God as Proverbs says, "in all your ways submit to him, and he will make your paths straight" (Prov. 3:6 NIV). The psalmist encourages us to "Commit your ways to the Lord; trust in him and he will do this" (Psalm 37:5 NIV). It's one thing to honor God when everything is going great for you. My question is whether we can we honor God when everything seems to be caving in all around us? true commitment to God (honor) comes out when everything else seems to be failing and caving in all around us. Let's honor God today in everything that we do. Honoring God is giving back to him what is rightfully his to begin with.

In your mind, what are some ways that you can think of that would honor God today? I have come to realize that when we honor God, it does not have to be something necessarily big that we do. We can honor him by the small things that we do when no one else sees except for God. When someone sees what we do, we can be recognized for it, but when only God sees what we do for him, he always receives honor for it. The question is as old as the Old Testament, "For I desire mercy, not sacrifice, and acknowledgment of God rather than burnt offerings" (Hos. 6:6 NIV). It is so awesome that God wants to know us. One of the ways God wants to know us is through us honoring him.

Launch Pad 3: Yield Your Ways for His Ways (Surrender Your Ways for His Ways

When we focus on our ways, we take our eyes off God and place our eyes on ourselves. Yielding means giving up something to gain something that is far better. That may seem like a prideful thing to say but let me explain. God really does want us to succeed. When he asks us to give up something it's because we don't need it and he has something far greater for us. We can't receive that new gift until we release the old thing God wants us to discard; think of it like that. When we yield, it's like a release from what weighs us down and yielding launches us into what he has for us. When we yield, we are asking God to take complete control. The definition of surrender is "Giving up self to authorities: an act of willing submission to authorities."[5] Surrender is an act of obedience, and fighting against the will of God is a dangerous thing to do. Your capacity to yield and surrender will determine your capacity to succeed.

Do I Have What It Takes to Make Something Out of My Life?

Be determined this day to take a stand for you and your family, a stand that declares that you will make something out of your life. Determined people will not quit even when everyone else quits.

When you are attempting to make something of your life, the easiest times to quit are either right before you make something out of your life or when there is no progress. Think of it like this: look at the Lord as your encourager, encouraging you to go forward, being your best support to make something out of your life. Jesus wants you to make something out of your life more than you want to make something out of your life. "Call to me, and I will answer you and tell you great and unsearchable things that you do not know" (Jeremiah. 33:3 NIV). Let me offer this explanation of this verse, "Call to me, and I will answer you" can be read as "Call to me, for I have many things to reveal to you about yourself that you do not know. Call to me, for I am eager and willing to answer you and to do great things in and through you. My kingdom will be imparted into others as you obey

40

me as I have commanded you to obey me." God wants to answer you.

The more you discover how to be the true to yourself, the more you realize that you have what it takes to make something out of your life. The more you discover who you are, the more you'll discover what you were created to be. John Maxwell says this amazing statement "true significance is only found by living in a relationship with God and by using one's energy and influence to pass along God's love to others."[6] The more you discover God, the more you will discover yourself. There are layers of unbelief that only the father can uncover for you. Some readers may believe they don't have the confidence or self-esteem to even begin to think they will ever have what it takes. I didn't either. Even if you are short on self-esteem you need to embrace and accept God's esteem for you.

I believe we have been blinded by a *myth* that has disabled our ability to believe in ourselves. The myth is this: What we have to offer won't work while what others do will cause them to make something out of their lives. The suggestion is that the focal point of our minds' lens has become so blinded that we can no longer see what we can do, so instead we're focused on what others can do, which takes the focus away from what we can do. A myth is something that is not true. But the more we focus on that myth, the more it becomes true.

It's still hard for me to believe that I do have what it takes to lead a life of significance because of all the deceptions I have allowed inside my heart and mind. I have allowed myself to become deceived and misled about who I truly am in God. I will explain more in the next chapter. When we receive deception about ourselves that we know is not true, we are opening ourselves up to something that was intended to mislead us. We can become so wrapped up in being misled that we don't even realize we are being misled. Ways that you become misled include surrounding yourself with people who will mislead you. Bad company will always corrupt good character. Bad company will also leave you feeling like you will not be able to accomplish anything. Character is a trait that you must attain to be a person of significance. Without having good character traits, such as honesty, respect, responsibility, and courage, there is no firm or stable foundation on which people can build on to help you do something great with your life.

When you feel like you don't have what it takes, ask God to reinforce for you that you *do* have what it takes. No one else can make you believe that you do have what it takes, except for you and God. The Lord has already determined your footsteps in everything that he created for you to do and for you to be. You were created for great value and great purpose. "In their hearts humans plans their course, but the Lord establishes their steps" (Prov. 16:9 NIV).

We may never have confidence in what we can do or have confidence we can be successful, but we can have

God's confidence inside of us. God confidence is the kind of confidence that says, "I can do all this through him who gives me strength" (Phil. 4:13 NIV). In today's language, Paul is telling us, "I can do what God has intended me to do. Through God's plans for my life, I will make something out of life." Has God called you to make something out of your life? *Yes!* Rise up out of the ashes of yesterday's failure and be confident! The Bible tells us, "Being confident of this, that he who began a good work in you will carry it on to completion until the day Christ Jesus" (Philippians 1:6 NIV). If Christ is confident in carrying on the completion of you, then you too can be in him.

To make something out of your life, you need to have the right kind of confidence. But we can go overboard in being confident in ourselves about accomplishing something, and that is when we become prideful. Being confident in your abilities to succeed is not wrong, but being prideful in your own abilities to attain significance *is* wrong.

Along your journey to discovering you, do what it takes to make something of yourself, don't quit! Another trap that we fall into is becoming paralyzed by fear because we allow past failure to cripple us to the point that we are no longer willing to even attempt to make something out of life. Fear is the opposite of courage. The Bible says that "For the spirit God gave us does not make us timid , but gives us power, love and self-disciple 2nd Timothy 1:7 NIV." Guess what? When you find yourself fearful, afraid that you will not be able to accomplish anything, only then can God accomplish something in and through you. "So he said to me, 'This is the word of the Lord to Zerubbabel: "Not by might nor by power, but by my Spirit"; says the Lord Almighty'" (Zechariah. 4:6 NIV). When you can't do it, only God can do it! What if you feel condemned by the mistakes and failures from past failed attempts to accomplish something? The Bible also says, "therefore, there is now no condemnation for those who are in Christ Jesus" (Romans 8:1 NIV). You have made it this far in your efforts to accomplish something out of your life, and I believe Jesus is saying, "Let me take you to a place of significance, a place that you cannot go yourself, but a place where only I can take you."

Do I have what it takes to be a man or a woman of God? That's a question that I believe is burning inside the heart of every man and every woman of God. and there is nothing wrong with asking that question. Being the true you Is much easier than being somebody that you're not. When we try to be someone that we are not, we end up not knowing if we have what it takes.

God is not done with you yet. If God was done with you, you wouldn't be here right now reading this book The insignificance that you feel right now is nothing in comparison to the significant life that God desires for you to live. Sometimes, God must break us to make us. Sometimes, God must allow us to go through times of feeling insignificant for us to feel significant in him.

There are many valleys of insignificance that we must walk through before we climb the summit to reach significance. Keep this prayerful thought close to your heart, Surely your goodness and love will follow me all of the days of my life, and I will dwell in the house of the Lord forever" (Psalms 23:6 NIV). Surely goodness and significance shall follow you; your God-given potential will support you when you feel like you can't do it. Listen to his voice as he calls you out of a life of insignificance and journey alongside him to live a life of significance.

The Bible tells us, "The Lord your God is with you, the Mighty Warrior who saves. He will take great delight in you; in his love he will no longer rebuke you but will rejoice over you with singing" (Zeph. 3:17 NIV). He is a hero who saves you. He happily rejoices over you, renews you with his love, and celebrates over you with shouts of joy. When no one else is with you, when everyone else tells you that you can't make something out of your life, when everyone else seems to be doing something with their life and you're not, always know the Lord your God is present.

We are all human and people will people fail people, but God will never fail us. By realizing that, I have been able to find out more and more about who I am and not allow what others to have said about me to destroy me and constantly bring me down. Your view of yourself determines everything. People can't determine what you do with your life unless you allow them to determine it for you. Make no mistake about it, we need people in our lives who will push us toward the direction we need to go, individuals who will speak life into us where others have spoken death to our circumstances. God places individuals in your life to help you receive blessing and council. Young people should listen to the instructions of father figures. My son, do not forget my teaching, but let your heart keep my commandments; 2 for length of days and years of life and peace they will add to you. (Proverbs 3:1–2 NIV). A father's instructions can determine everything in the young and old. That is why it is very important that you find father figures who will invest in you, who will speak into your circumstances, who will speak life where there is no life.

If we could learn how to speak life into any situation, could also learn how to avoid the negative things that we continue to allow to hold us back. them... We have become so used to being somebody else we are not that I am afraid that we've lost the value of being true to yourself. nobody wants to be somebody they are not. My hope is that, through reading the second chapter of this book, my readers will begin to be released from past failures; that readers will be released from every mistake of trying to be somebody that they are not, and instead run in their true God-given freedom to be who they truly are and who they are truly meant to be. When we finally get to the point of being freed from the past, we can live life to the fullest and receive all that God has intended for us to receive. Everything that was meant to be is in your hands and no one can take it from you unless you give them permission to take it.

The best way to help someone be their true self is to confront them through positive reinforcements that cause them to look deep within themselves, which will help them realize that there is something great within them. A positive reinforcement always brings out the best in people and causes people to begin to believe in themselves. When you reinforce something positive in someone's life, you are giving them the ability and the strength to do something positive with their life.

As I have been writing this chapter, I have come to realize that I am still figuring out how to be true to myself and be the true me. I also have come to realize that it's okay if I haven't figured out yet how to be fully true to myself and be the true me. The same is true for you. You can be true to yourself and be the true you.

Let's Pray:

Lord, we are overcomers through you and in you. God, help us to remain true to ourselves, as you have created us to be. Lord, you didn't create us to be anyone else except ourselves. In Jesus's name, Amen.

3

Only You Can Be You

Sow to yourselves in righteousness, reap in mercy; break up your fallowed ground: for it is time to seek the Lord, until he comes and rain righteousness upon you.
—Hosea 10:12 NIV

We have allowed ourselves to become so rooted in the daily struggles of life trying to figure out who we are that we have allowed the roots and thorns and thistles that entangle us to the point where we lose who we are.

Learn to love yourself before you are loving others. It is so easy to find people who walk around disliking themselves, which causes them to dislike others, because they do not love themselves. Learning to be a person of significance starts with loving yourself and believing in yourself. No one has ever gained something without first learning to love themselves.

There are so many ways we confine ourselves by giving ourselves excuses to not love ourselves. For a long time, I struggled with believing in and loving myself and that left me crippled in seeing my own potential. I didn't see the potential in myself that others saw. Several years ago, I was setting up chairs for youth group and saw my reflection in the chair. I can't remember exactly how I asked God, but I asked him something like "What do you see in my reflection?" The words, "My beloved son," came to my mind. You see, for the longest time I couldn't come to grips with loving myself and accepting myself. In fact, I still struggle with loving and accepting myself. It blows my mind that God loves me for being me. Remember that God loves you for being you.

Scripture tells us: "For God so loved the world, that he gave his only begotten Son, that whoever believes in him shall not perish, but have eternal life.17 For God did not send the son into the world to judge the world, but that the world might be saved through him." (John 3:16–17 NIV). A key to learning how to love yourself before you love others is realizing how much God loves and cares for you. Humanity will always have one thing in common with each other, and that is the longing to be loved. Sadly, we have lost the value of loving and accepting ourselves for who we are, and I think we base our love and acceptance of ourselves on how others perceive how we should be.

God designed you to be you. You have characteristics that no one else has that distinguishes you from everybody else. When you are the real you, no one else can take away you except for you. Jesus said: "Love the Lord your God with all your heart and with all your soul and all your mind" (Matt. 22:37 NIV). This verse is a key to learning how to love yourself before you love others, which is to first love the Lord with all your heart, all your soul, and all your mind. These three components are crucial to loving yourself., Jesus says, "A new command I give you: Love one another. As I have loved you, so must you love one another" (John 13:34 NIV).

The journey of being you begins now. You are the only one who can be you. Forget about what has happened in the past, and instead push forward to the future. In Isaiah 43 we read, "Forget the former things; do not dwell on the past" (Isa. 43:18 NIV). One of the pitfalls to discovering that you can be you is by dwelling on the former things, on what others have said about you. Words marked me for so long that I've allowed myself to become what others said I was, instead of me discovering me to be me. you find out who you are, it is so much easier for you to begin to love yourself and to love others.

The Wounded Soul

Reason 1: A fatherless generation has left its mark on society and has left thousands, if not millions, wounded and they are not becoming who they were meant to be. God did not create duplicates, though God is "A father to the fatherless, a defender of widows, is God in his holy dwelling" (Psalm 68:5 NIV). Today we see too many in our society with wounded souls not being themselves, the "you" God intended. The Bible tells us, "Religion that God our Father accepts as pure and faultless is this: to look after orphans and widows in their distress and to keep oneself from being polluted by the world" (James 1:27 NIV).

You no longer have to be held captive by a wounded soul. The reason so many walk around wounded, not knowing their God-given identity and not knowing who they are in Christ, is because we have failed to equip them to be fully themselves. It's time that we see the invading atmosphere of heaven coming like a mighty rushing wind to see wounded souls healed, so we can continue our journey to significance. It's time that we, as co-laborers of Christ, carry the gift of significance to those who feel insignificant.

I believe there is a shift coming. The tide is beginning to turn. The hearts of fathers are beginning to be turned toward the hearts of sons and daughters who have lost their significance. Therefore, if anyone is in Christ, the new creation has come: The old has gone, the new is here!" (2 Corinthians 5:17 NIV). If we believe this, then why are we constantly walking around in our old garments, in our old ways when we are new in him and through him? Christian or non-Christian, your background doesn't matter. If are carrying past hurt and allowing it to inform your decisions now, you will be held back by the past, and that wound will never be able to receive its full healing.

Reason 2: Forgive and forget; no longer will you labor in the past. The more you labor on the wound, the more open the wound becomes. Unforgiveness is a weapon that the enemy has unleashed like never before. Until you learn to forgive others, you will never be able to forgive yourself. Until you are willing to forgive the wound, the wound cannot heal. When you forgive others, you forgive yourself. When you can come to forgiveness, your wound will begin to heal, and you will be able to walk now as God directs you, walking into only you that you can be you. There has to be reason people walk around every day with their heads down and their souls crying out with a longing to find out who they are. Scripture offers this prayer:

> And forgive us our debts, as we also have forgiven our debtors. 13 And lead us not into temptation, but deliver us from the evil one. 14 For if you forgive other people when they sin against you, your heavenly Father will also forgive you. 15 But if you do not forgive others their sins, your Father will not forgive your sins. (Matthew 6:12–15 NIV)

Let's break these four verses down. The first verse is saying that each time we hold on to a debt rooted in something that someone said against us, the more you take ownership of that debt, which causes it to become our debt that we carry. Could it be that thousands of people feel insignificant because they have bought debts that belong to others who have spoken ill or otherwise wrongful words about them? In the next verse we see the temptation is to continue speaking the lies others spoke about you, the debts that you have bought from others. To overcome, put a guard around your mind, around your heart, to withstand the temptation. The Bible contains everything you need to know to speak life over yourself and others, everything you need to know to cancel the debt that you have bought from the word's others have spoken about you, and everything you need to know about withstanding temptations. In the next verse we discover that forgiveness is not determined by an outward expression. Forgiveness is expressed through inward expression. It's easy for us to believe that we have forgiven someone because of the outward expression, while we are still wounding ourselves by remaining unforgiving. Continuing to refuse forgiveness to someone inwardly harms only yourself. We will not be released into being the "only you that you can be you" until we learn how to give forgiveness of ourselves for our own mistakes and forgiveness of those who have done wrong to us. Every time you refuse to forgive yourself or to forgive others, you're giving up your right to be forgiven by the father. A person of significance is a person of forgiveness who expresses forgiveness and, through the release of forgiveness, allows their wounded soul to heal. I understand that the greater the wound is the more difficult it is for someone to forgive; however, which do you prefer, to continue to carry around the baggage of a wounded soul or to experience freedom and healing of the wounded soul and continue your journey to significance? The choice is yours. You must choose by faith to either forgive and be forgiven or to remain unforgiving and suffer the consequence of a wounded soul.

Reason 3 Choose self-acceptance knowing people will fail you. Those who are close to you will fail you. The only one who will never fail you is God. I have had to come to realize that people will fail me, but God will never fail me. We put walls up around our wounds, the wounds of our past hurts caused by people who have failed us, and we can't trust anyone anymore because of the hurts caused by those who failed us. We form our identities based on what others say about us. So, if anyone says something hurtful to us it triggers the past wound, which causes us to compromise. Self-acceptance is necessary at these times. Until you learn how to accept yourself for who you are, no one else will be able to completely accept you for who you are. Man's approval will only get you so far. God's approval will get you as far as you're willing to go in him.

See yourself as God created you to be. Man has always based his approval on man's approval. In Matthew 6 we read, "Do not store up for yourselves treasures on earth, where moths and vermin destroy, and where thieves break in and steal. But store up for yourselves treasures in heaven, where moths and vermin do not destroy, and where thieves do not break in and steal. For where your treasure is, there your heart will be also" (Matt. 6:19–21 NIV). We care so much about what others say about us that we begin to store those things inside of us. If we are not careful these things will destroy us as we journey to significance. You are not bound by people's opinions of how you live your life, so be freed this day of the chains of bondage that have held the wounded soul in bondage. Walk now into the deliverer's hand and live a significant life free of the wounded soul. Before you buy into what others say about you, always look to what God says about you. The Bible says in Deuteronomy 28:13 that you are the head and not the tail that you are above and not beneath. People did not choose you; God chose you first. You are a royal priesthood in the kingdom. Believe God, "Do not be misled: 'Bad company corrupts good character'" (1 Cor. 15:33 NIV).

Habits vs. Attitudes

To live a significant life, we have to live a life based on a higher standard than the world's values. We must conform to a higher standard, God's standard. To live in significance, what you do in the unseen, where no one else is looking, truly defines your significance. We must live by the fruits of the Spirit.

> *But the fruit of the Spirit is* love, joy, peace, patience, kindness, goodness, faithfulness, gentleness and self-control. *Against such things there is no law.*
> —Galatians 5:22–23 NIV (emphasis mine)

How we respond tells how we are in our character how we react tells how we are in our attitudes. The greater significance the deeper our character and attitudes need to be anchored. Without character, life will fail. John Maxwell says it this way that "Character and integrity are the glue that holds everything together in life."[7] John Maxwell character quote

The second greatest commandment in the Bible is to love your neighbor as yourself. In order to sustain a life of significance, we must first learn how to n order to see his motives for our lives. It's easy to love someone when everything is going well; it's far more difficult to love someone when everything is going wrong. Significant people must deal with people's stuff every day. That's just a part of life. I love this quote by John Maxwell: "People don't care how much you know until they see how much you care."[8] Humanity—from young to old to Christian to non-Christian—is crying out in desperation "Would you love me despite my 'stuff'?

Character is what you do when no one else is looking. Habits play a role in forming of character. Have circumstances ever shaped your attitude toward something? Or has a habit ever developed out of a circumstance whether it was inside your control or outside your control? How has that habit benefited you?

A life of significance must be aligned with the proper character and attitudes. People can't trust you without first knowing what you stand for and whether your character is in line with God's truth.

Attitude is one of the main attributes of a person that people are attracted to. What is truly on the inside of an individual will be seen when everything is going against them. Some of the most significant people in the world are also some of the most miserable people in the world because their character does not match their habits, and their attitude is just an outward appearance, not an inward appearance The Bible says that man looks to the outward appearance, but God looks at the inward appearance; God looks at the heart. Our appearance will always reflect our habits and attitudes.

Love

There is no fear in love. But perfect love drives out fear, because fear has to do with punishment. The one who fears is not made perfect in love. (1 John 4:18 NIV). Will we allow our attitudes to get in the way of loving others? I could be wrong—please forgive me if I am—but I think almost every religion goes by the principle.

"Love your neighbor as yourself" (Matt. 22:39 NIV). How we love one another is often revealed through our attitudes. Love is the weapon that breaks down all walls. Love breaks down all generational curses. Love causes people to go out their way to help others. Love is a significant feature that needs to be shown in today's culture. "Greater love has no one than this: to lay down one's life for one's friends. (John 15:13 NIV).

Joy

People can tell between a fake and someone who walks it out. This generation and the coming generations need to see the joy that only comes from above. When everything is going wrong and nothing is going right, the Bible says, "The LORD is my strength and my shield; my heart trusts in him, and he helps me. My heart leaps for joy, and with my song I praise him" (Psalm 28:7 NIV). It's one thing to produce joy when everything is going great, but it's a whole different story to produce the joy of the Lord when all hell is breaking out against you.

If you ever encounter someone that acted in a way that made you recognize that there was something different about their life? It's because they live L.I.F.E., which means to Live In Fullness Every day. I don't know about you, but I don't want to allow my attitudes or habits to rob me of the fullness of life that I can live every day. You can be joyful and still not have everything together. You can have joy instead of depression during the chaos of life.

Peace

Peace I leave with you; my peace I give you. I do not give to you as the world gives. do not let your hearts be troubled and do not be afraid" (John 14:27 NIV). Christ's peace is an everlasting peace. His peace is with you in the midst of the storms of life. The Bible says, "Do not be anxious about anything, but by prayer and petition, with thanksgiving present your requests to God. And the peace of God which transcends all understanding will guard your hearts and your minds in Christ Jesus" (Phil. 4:6–7 NIV). The peace of God is what guides us. I will never forget the day my mom got out of the hospital after having quadruple bypass surgery. The moment I reached the top of the hill to get to where I lived, the wind started blowing; and, to me, it was as if God was breathing the winds of heaven, he was breathing his peace into my life. There are two different kinds of peace, an outward peace and an inward peace. Outward peace always looks at the circumstances when an inward peace always looks to the circumstance solver.

Patience

I am not a patient person at all. I want things to happen all at once and when I think it's the right timing. Patience is the key that produces perseverance, and it is one of the greatest teachers in life. Learning to be patient is formed by our habits and attitudes. Have you ever noticed what being impatient can do to you? I sure have. I have noticed that when I become impatient and when I want to take more control, I have the tendency to mess up more.

Kindness

It only takes one kind word to make someone's day; it also only takes on wrong word to ruin someone's day. We can make or break people every day by the attitudes that we display to them. I know, for me, many times I have this mentality that says, *well, I am going to give them a piece of my mind and tell them what I think of them.* Maybe you are the same. If so, before we react let's make sure to first show kindness to someone, no matter what the circumstance. Sometimes, we have too love the hell out of people and show direct kindness to them through their circumstances.

Goodness

The Bible says, "Surely your goodness and love will follow me all the days of my life, and I will dwell in the house of the LORD forever" (Psalm 23:6 NIV).

I believe that inside everyone there is a measure of goodness, but we are the ones who must pull it out of them. It's the goodness of the father that causes his love and mercy to follow you all the days of your life. For those of you reading this who feel like they are not good enough to succeed in life, I issue you this challenge: *Proclaim* the promise of this verse and *reclaim* this promise over your lifetime again and again until it becomes stuck inside of you.

Faithfulness

We live in a culture that announces unfaithfulness and denounces faithfulness. No one gets anywhere in life by being unfaithful. People get somewhere in life by being faithful. I believe divorce would end if we could learn to be faithful. It's been proven that if we can't be faithful in the small things, we will never remain faithful in the bigger things in life. The greatest leaders in our culture and society today are those who have remained faithful. I believe the key to building anything successful, from home life to a business, from a ministry to a friendship, is to remain faithful in the small things God wants you to remain faithful in the now—not later. Being faithful in the now will prepare you to be faithful in the later.

Gentleness

Our body language tells everything about us. How we interact with people will determine how people view us. Gentleness is this having a gracious and honorable way you carry yourself. I believe the more significant a person becomes the more influence they have and the greater the demand is for them to be a gentle person because of the people who look up to them. The Bible says that a gentle rebuke is like medicine to the bones, but a harsh rebuke is a crushing blow. Gentleness will always begin on the inside and flows from the inside to the outside of an individual. Which is more valuable to listen to, a harsh person or a person who is gentle and humble?

Self-Control

The Bible tells us, "You, dear children, are from God and have overcome them, because the one who is in you is greater than the one who is in the world" (1 John 4:4 NIV).

Self-control is knowing when to have something and when to not have something. Self-control is knowing when to speak up and when not to not speak up, and control the tongue, Self-control is knowing when to do something and when not to do something.

Greatness Is Inside Each of Us

We all have self-inflicted wounds, and we will never be able to see the greatness inside of us until we learn how to develop our greatness through the greater one who lives within us. The greatness inside of us will never be achieved through a prideful manner. Instead, greatness will be achieved through humility as we journey to significance. Greatness will never be seen through what everybody sees you doing. Greatness will be seen in what others don't see you doing, that will carry you into what you do where everybody sees you differently. As you continue to seek to be the better, your results will start to show up. No one sees someone else struggling to stick to a daily diet, but in time they can start seeing the results in the diet. The same is true for you. Keep moving forward in doing what you are doing daily to develop habits that will produce results that everyone can see.

Greatness is not built on the foundation of success: success is built on the foundation of greatness through a life of humility. Understand this: the more greatness you have in your significance, the more conflict you have. How you carry yourself in daily life determines how well you will be able to handle greatness through significance in influencing others. Matthew 23 says, "The greatest among you will be your servant. For those who exalt themselves will be humbled, and those who humble themselves will be exalted" (Matt. 23:11–12 NIV). Greatness is not about how much you will be exalted or how much you seek to be exalted. Greatness is about putting others before yourself.

For what are you using the greatness within you?

If we use our greatness for self-gain, we will lose everything. If we use it for kingdom gain, we will gain everything that God has entrusted to us. Our choice to use our greatness for self or for his kingdom will determine how much more he can trust us with. The world has been buying into greatness, but that has nothing to do with how talented you are. It has to do with how you use those talents and how faithful you are with those talents; that's what makes greatness in the journey to significance.

> His master replied, "Well done, good and faithful servant! You have been faithful with a few things; I will put you in charge of many things. Come and share your master's Happiness! 22 The man with two bags of gold also came. "Master; he said,'you entrusted me with two bags of gold; see, I have gained two more. 23 His master replied, 'Well done, good and faithful servant! You have been faithful with a few things; I will put you in charge of many things. Come and share your master's happiness!' (Matthew 25:21–23 NIV)

The Bible is full of stories of people who continued to pursue their God-given greatness. Imagine there is a container right beside you that contains all your God-given abilities, and on the other side of that container is another container filled with everything that reminds you of your past, which contains all the reasons you're not qualified to receive the greatness and uniqueness that God has blessed you with. The container that contains everything that God has for you is only found and opened by these four things:

1. By getting into his word to meditate on him daily.

2. By having daily communication with him throughout the day.

3. By living a life that brings honor to him.

4. By serving.

Getting Into His Word

By getting into his word and meditating on him. "I have hidden your word in my heart that I may not sin against you" (Psalm 119:11 NIV). you build yourself up daily by being a student of the word of God and that prepares you for everything that God has for you. Greatness is not seen in what you do; greatness is seen in what you do when no one else sees except for you and God. Greatness is found within the scriptures. Dive in and capture the greatness for yourself along your journey.

Daily Communication

"But seek first his kingdom and his righteousness, and all these things will be given to you as well" (Matt. 6:33 NIV). The kingdom's purpose for your life is only found when you seek first his agenda for your life instead of your own agenda. The most important action that you can take to live a life of greatness is to do what he wants you to do. Greatness says, "I will lay down my wants for his wants." Greatness says, "Forget about me; instead, look to the king and his kingdom to pursue the greatest thing of all, and that is his kingdom and righteousness."

Living a Life That Honors Him

A life that honors God is also a life that pleases God. You don't have to be perfect to honor him. A simple way to honor God is by coming to him just as you are, just as he created you to be. Whoever serves me must follow me; and where I am, my servant also will be. My Father will honor the one who serves me. (John 12:26 NIV). Live a life that honors and serves the king and his purposes.

Serve Him

One of the greatest ways to elevate your significance is by being a servant to other people. If you can make serving others a daily lifestyle, it will elevate you into a higher level. 26 Not so with you. Instead, whoever wants to become great among you, must be your servant, 27 and whoever wants to be first must be your slave. 28 Just as the son of man did not come to be served, but to serve, and to give his life a ransom for many (Matthew 20:26–28 NIV).

Let's look at your imaginary container filled with the regrets, the failures, and the mistakes of your past—the limitations in your life. By the way, you don't have to live by that container and continue to have it opened in your life. The only one who can make that choice not to live by that container is you.

- Reminders: every time we allow ourselves to come close enough to that container, we give ourselves the memo where that the reminders of our regrets are written, which causes us to relive them every day. Ultimately, these reminders steal away any potential of us seeing the great things that God has for us.

- Failures: Let's get this straight from the beginning: You're not a failure; you're a winner in the kingdom of God. There are no failures; there are only winners. One of the ways the enemy will tempt you to open that container, or to come close enough to that container to be tempted to open it, is by deceiving you and making you believe that you are a failure.

- Mistakes: Maybe, like me, you have made a lot of mistakes that cause you to get close to your container of mistakes. Participating in reliving these mistakes causes psychological damage that includes making you believe that you will continue making mistakes. Run from that container that feeds you those lies and causes you to live in them. Once you ask for forgiveness of those mistakes, the king no longer remembers them, and the same should be true for you. The king gives you the strength to rise above that container and declare, "I am not a mistake!"

- Limitations: We all have them, we all face them, and we all struggle with them. When we focus on them every day, limitations will cause us to come up short every time, and we will fall short of what God has planned for us. Why is it that we always focus on what we can't do instead of focusing on what we can do? Choosing to focus on the things we can't do limits us; it keeps us from doing the various things that we can do. Scripture

69

tells us, "I can do all this through him who gives me strength. (Philippians. 4:13 NIV). Therefore, everything that God has called you to do, you can do. Through his strength, you can successfully use every talent he has granted you.

Seize the moment where you are now, before you seize the dream of where you can be.

It is important that we develop the mentality that says I will seize every day as another opportunity to learn and to grow. One of the greatest ways to seize the moment right where you are is by writing it down. As the Bible says, "Then the Lord replied:" Write down the revelation and make it plain on tablets so that a herald may run with it. ' (Habakkuk. 2:2 NIV) "Where there is no revelation, people cast off restraint; but blessed is the one who heeds wisdom's instruction. (Proverbs. 29:18 NIV). There is something inside each of us that is driven by a vision that can steer us and drive us into our moments of where we are to go.

It's easy to seize the moment now, but it's not easy to seize the dream of where we can be. We live in a culture that screams out to see the bigger picture of life. The bigger picture is only seen through the lens of seizing the moment now and taking it day by day. Step by step, the vision for your life in your journey to significance can be more clearly seen if you can stay with the vision by taking care of the now and not taking care of the later.

The advantage of seizing the moment now is that you began to develop and cultivate your resources now for seizing your dream later. Our dreams can be undeveloped because of not seizing the moment now.

Determine now the moments that you will seize. Every great achiever in life was great at seizing their moment. Success is not measured by how much you have achieved. Success is measured by how you seized the moment to achieve your success. Learn to save your moments to seize your moments. No one has ever seized a dream without first becoming proactive in everything that they do and put their hands to.

Wherever there is an opportunity, there will always be a moment to seize. I believe that there is at least one opportunity to be seized. God sets up divine moments for us every day to seize. It's up to us to recognize those divine moments. When you seize your moment, it's totally up to you in what you do with your moment. The choices you make in seizing those moments will always impact the outcome of seizing your dream, John Maxwell says "leadership is influence."[9] I believe that significance is also influence. People will be influenced one way or another by you seizing your moment. " In their hearts humans plan their course, but the Lord establishes their steps." (Proverbs. 16:9 NIV). It's so easy to have envision our lives planned out without the Lord first determining us steps.

Our dreams and visions would have a higher impact on people's lives every day if we could learn to let go of our agendas for his agenda for our lives.

We must check our motives every day regarding the goals that we want to achieve and in the moments that we seize. "All a person's ways seem pure to them, but motives are weighed by the Lord. (Proverbs. 16:2 NIV). It is easy for us to be so caught up in our own motives that we lose sight of the kingdom purposes and ignore that the king plants his motives inside each of our hearts. We must refocus our motives to have our motives and fix them upon his motives.

For This is what the Lord Almighty says: "After the Glorious One sent me against the nations that have plundered you—for whoever touches you touches the apple of his eye " (Zechariah. 2:8 NIV). It's amazing to me that God sees great value in us. The creator of the world saw fit to specifically tell us as individuals that he sees great value in us "Before I formed you in the womb I knew you, before you were born, I set you apart" (Jer. 1:5). He knew us even before we knew ourselves. God was already at work in our lives during conception. God saw your unformed body in your mother's womb. and said, Don't ever allow the enemy to steal away your great value that God sees in you, and that I have planted inside of your unformed body."

When the circumstances today seem to steal away your value, remember this: Never. look at the circumstance.

Instead, look to the circumstance solver. "14 I praise you because I am fearfully and wonderfully made; your works are wonderful; I know that full well. 15 My frame was not hidden from you when I was made in the secret place, when I was woven together in the depths of the earth. 16 Your eyes saw my unformed body; all the days ordained for me were written in your book before one of them came to be" (Psalm 139:14-16 NIV). An interesting thought, isn't it, that you are on God's mind every day? The creator of the universe thinks about you every day "How precious also are your thoughts towards me, God, how vast is the sum of them!" (Psalm 139:17 NIV). Whenever you are down, look at yourself in the mirror, and declare over yourself that God sees great value in you. Repeat it until it becomes a part of you, Why, my soul, are you downcast? Why so disturbed within me? Put your hope in God, for I will yet praise him, my savior and my God!" (Psalm 42:5NIV). The greatest source of protecting your value is proclaiming your value. The Bible says that life and death are in the power of the tongue. The greatest weapon the enemy will use to take away your value is yourself. Have you ever noticed that the more you say that you don't have any value, the more you steal away your value.

When you think of value, what is that you picture? Let's look at three things that the secular world view as valuable.

- **Money, Possessions:** Human nature says the more money and possessions you have, the more value you will have in people's eyes. To an extent, that could be true if the money were generated in the proper way. "For the love of money is the root of all kinds of evil. Some people, eager for money, have wandered from the faith and pierced themselves with griefs. 11 But you, man of God, flee from all this, and pursue righteousness, godliness, faith, love, endurance and gentleness. 12 Fight the good fight of the faith. Take hold of the eternal life to which you were called when you made your good confession in the presence of many witnesses. (1 Timothy 6:10-12 NIV). Money and possessions can be good and beneficial if they don't take away the value between you and God, and they add value to others. Think about the money that is generated all over the world. Where does this money add value to more, to human gratifications or to serving the poor and adding value to those who have felt like that they have lost their value? **Pride**

"Pride goes before destruction, a haughty spirit before the fall" (Proverbs. 16:18 NIV)

We live in a culture where it's human nature to say, "It's all about me;" where we fall into the trap of boasting about ourselves and our accomplishments without giving honor where honor is due. But he gives more grace. That is why Scripture says: 'God opposes the proud, but shows favor to the humble." (James 4:6 NIV).

Being Morally Incorrect

"The Lord watches over the foreigner and sustains the fatherless and the widow, but he frustrates the ways of the wicked" (Psalm 146:9 NIV).

God's values have always been different from human societies', especially the society in which we live today. We must always be careful where we place our value and find our value. Society's moral values have decreased so much that everyday thousands of parents are getting divorced. No longer do we see value in what's right and what's wrong. Instead, we have switched around right and wrong. Wrong is now what is right, what's right is now what's wrong. But there is a better end to this story. God is restoring the values today to be what he values through his kingdom restores. True value can be seen from the inside out. God has instilled value in each of us. We are so valued by God that we are created in his likeness. "So God created mankind in his own image, in the image of God he created them; male and female he created them" (Gen. 1:27 NIV).

"But the lord said to Samuel, 'Do not consider his appearance or his height, for I have rejected him. The Lord does not look at the things that man looks at. People look at the outward appearance, but the LORD looks at the heart" (1 Samuel 16:7 NIV).

Let's look at three things in which God sees value.

First, God always loves a cheerful giver, not giving out of obligation, but giving out of pure. obedience toward God. 2 Corinthians 9:7-8 Each of you should give what you have decided in your heart to give, not reluctantly or under compulsion, for God loves a cheerful giver. 8 And God is able to bless you abundantly, so that in all things at all times, having all that you need, you will abound in every good work" (2 Corinthians 9:7–8 NIV). This principle has been used throughout history. It's not just a principle of giving money, it's also a principle of being a cheerful giver of your time, of your talents, and many other things that delights the heart of God when you are cheerful in giving. Some of the best ways to give is by giving someone what they deserve, and that is the love of God.

God Sees Value in Unity

I in them and you in me – so that they May be brought to complete unity. Then the world will know that you sent me and have loved them even as you have loved me?" (John 17:23 NIV). I believe being unified as one is what will break the cycle of many of the problems that we all face in our cultures today. Think of it like this: If society, church and families can be disrupted, it is like a domino effect.

God Always Sees Value in Caring for the Fatherless Orphan, the Widow, and the Poor.

"Religion that God our Father accepts as pure and faultless is this: to look after orphans and widows in their distress and to keep oneself from being polluted by the world" (James 1:27 NIV). I believe the most single significant impact that you can make on another person's life is by caring for the fatherless, the orphan, the widow, and the poor. Nothing else is closer to the father's heart than that: The spirit of the Sovereign Lord is on me, because the Lord has anointed me to proclaim the good news to the poor. He has sent me to bind up the brokenhearted, and to proclaim freedom for the captives and release from darkness for the prisoners, **2** to proclaim the year of the Lord's favor and the day of vengeance of our God, to comfort all who mourn" (Isaiah 61:1–2 NIV).

Who Am I?

This question has been asked and repeated throughout the ages. Men and women have sought to find out who they are and why they were created. There's even a popular song, "History Maker" written by Martin Smith.[10]

The lyrics go something like this: "I want to be a history maker, a truth speaker to all mankind." Inside of you lives a history maker who is longing to ask this question: "Who am I God? Let's look at some of these questions. Who you are is not who you were in the past, but who you are today. Let's start out every day by declaring that we are not a mistake; we are winners.

Question 1: Why was I created? The whole intention of this book is to make a difference in your life, so you, in turn, can make a difference in someone else's life. Think about it: there are certain things that only you can do, things that no one else can do, and that's what makes you who are you are. Has it ever run through your mind that there has to be a reason, a purpose, a plan as to why I was created and why I am still alive and standing today? It's okay to ask "Why was I created?" but it's not okay to buy into that question and allow the question to become a debt to you, causing you to think that you were created for nothing. The Bible tells us that God's word is sharper than a double-edged sword. May his word cut through the lie of feeling like a mistake in life. If you feel like that, read Romans chapter 8 again and again until it becomes a part of you. Make that announcement over yourself that in Christ alone you are more than a conqueror.

Question 2: God, why do I feel like I can't amount to anything? Allow the heart of God to be spoken into your

heart. I have seen the tears. I have seen the hidden heartache that no one else sees, for I am with you. Never forget
that you were made in the Lord's own image and no one
else can take that away from you except for you. For my
word was sent forth from the beginning of time for you,
for I have not forgotten about you. For I am creating in you
a whole heart, and I am taking what was once a bitter and
broken past and turning your future into beauty for ashes.
Hidden insecurities will no longer hold you bounded, be
free from the chains of the shattered pieces of a broken
heart that has been wounded to the point of feeling so
insecure that you can't amount to anything be encouraged and rest in his freedom. I can still remember as if it
happened yesterday. Until I was around the age of twen-
ty-two or twenty-four, I was so crippled by the thoughts
of worthlessness that I never thought I would amount to
anything. Today I am twenty-seven, and I have a lot of
dreams. One of my dreams is to write books. Allow God
to speak to your heart, and through the power of Christ
let's denounce the crippling deceptions that we have fallen
prey to that tell us that we will never amount to anything.
Say it with me:

I denounce feeling worthless, and I announce over my
life once more that I have worth in my life. I denounce
the crippling thoughts of the insecurities of today, and I
announce over my life this day the security of love that
comes from Abba Father. I denounce every part in us that
feels insignificant, and I declare in Jesus's name that you

are significant. We break the chains. We break the generational curses of depression and insecurities that have crippled us. Be free and walk in him. Predetermine this day that you can and will walk as a winner and overcome the obstacles and hurdles that you face every day. The reason we feel like we can't amount to anything is because we have already predetermined that we can't amount to anything.

Question 3: Who am I in your eyes, God? I think if we are all honest, we have all asked God, "Who am I in your eyes?" Not only do I believe we have all asked that question, but we have also asked that question to friends, relatives, and ourselves. Something I've learned is it is all about how you view yourself. The lens you view your life through is that same lens that others will use to view your life. Did you know that God knew you even during conception? The best way to get to know who you are in the eyes of the father, is by getting to know him first.

Let's Pray:

Father, reveal to us what is truly means to be who you have created us to be. Lord Jesus may our priority always be to bring honor to you, in only you can be you, as you have created us to be. Holy Spirit may you release a fresh touch into lives with the DNA of heaven that you have created us to be as individuals.

4

A Road Less Traveled

13 Enter through the narrow gate. for wide is the gate and broad is the road that leads to destruction, And many l enter through it 14 But small is the gate and narrow the road that leads to life, and only a few find it.
—Matthew 7:13–14 NIV

A road less traveled is the path that very few have had the courage to embark. It's a path that, if you take it, you begin to realize that you can't travel on it by yourself on your own strength. It's the path that you take that will cost you something to travel on it. It is also the path on which you gain something far greater than you ever imagined. Throughout history no one ever traveled on this road without paying a price. Throughout this chapter as we take this journey. ask yourself what you can do to travel on the road less traveled.

There were three travelers on the road less traveled. The first traveler was confident he was ready for the road less traveled, The second traveler traveled with humility and prepared years ahead of time for this journey that was right in front of him. The third traveler traveled the road looking beyond himself to see into someone else's need.

The Message

30-32 Jesus answered by telling a story. "There was once a man traveling from Jerusalem to Jericho. On the way he was attacked by robbers. They took his clothes, beat him up, and went off leaving him half-dead. Luckily, a priest was on his way down the same road, but when he saw him he angled across the to the other side, Then a Levite religious man showed up, he also avoided the injured man.33-35 A Samaritan traveling the same road came on him. when he saw the man's condition, his heart went out to him. He gave him first aid, disinfecting and bandaging his wounds. The he lifted him onto his donkey, led him to an inn, And made him comfortable, in the morning he took out two silver coins and gave them to the innkeeper, saying, "Take good care of him. If it costs any more, put it on my bill-I'll pay you on my way back." 36 "What do you think? Which of these three became a neighbor to the man attacked by robbers? 37 "The one who treated him kindly," the religion scholar responded. Jesus said, "Go and do the same." (Luke 10:30–37 The Message)

Traveler 1—On any road that we travel, if we become too confident in our strengths, we can become complacent and not recognize what it is that we are meant to accomplish on this road. How often is it that when we are a traveler on a road, we pass people by who are in need and, though their need is right before our eyes, we move over and pass by them on the other side of the road? We unconsciously judge their need to see if it meets our standards. The greatest standard we can set for ourselves is a standard set to see people where they are, so our expectations for them can be higher. A road less traveled is not fit for traveler one, who will always see the need before they ever see what benefits them. It's easy to take care of the need when everybody else is looking. It's a lot more difficult to take care of the need when no one else is looking. Something that I have been challenged with, and honestly struggle with, is taking care of the need that is before me when no one else is looking. I feel like the priest who crosses over to the other side of the need.

Traveler 2—When we pass up the need of another we can see with our own eyes and we know we can do something about it, we give ourselves the excuse that someone else can take care of need that we could have taken of. Seriously, He observed the situation from far away and decided that he didn't want the responsibility of taking care of a wounded man and that someone else could take care of him.

The Road of Obstacles and Hurdles

Along the road less traveled, anything that was gained without obstacles or hurdles was never really gained. Every day we have the choice to either take the easy road or to take the hard road. Travelers who choose the easy road do so looking out for themselves. Travelers on the difficult road, the road less traveled, put others first. Every day across America and the world people travel the road less traveled. Throughout this chapter, I want to highlight some people who have traveled this road and have seen humanity awakened. It's not necessary to travel around the world to see humanity awakened, because awakening occurs on the road less traveled; and it's not necessary to travel around the world to travel this road, it's right where you are. When you care for your family, neighbors, friends, and local strangers, you are traveling the less-traveled road. In fact, caring for those close to you is training ground.

Have you watched the hurdle races at a track meet or in the Olympics? Those who run the hurdle races have trained ahead of time in preparation. This way, they know how and when to jump over the hurdles. The same is true for us. We must prepare and train ourselves ahead of time, so when the hurdles do come, we can win our race. "Do not be deceived: God cannot be mocked. A man reaps what he sows" (Galatians. 6:7 NIV).

How often does it happen in everyday life that people, me included, get tripped up by life's hurdles, when, if we would have prepared ahead of time, we could have leaped over them? The road of obstacles and hurdles is not meant to bring out the worst in you; it's meant to bring out the best in you. It's been said that the more significant you are, the lonelier the road is.

The reason very few travels on this road is because it will cost them something to travel on this road. Nothing in life is ever gained without it first costing something. Have you ever noticed that the more you do, the greater impact you have, the lonelier you are? The void of loneliness will never be filled by what you do, or by who you know. The cure to filling loneliness is by getting to the root cause of why you feel that way. Loneliness is a byproduct of relationship; relationship is what will buy out loneliness every time. Again, and I can't emphasize this enough, significance will never be found in what you do or who you know; significance begins on the inside and is rooted in who you *are*.

I realize that those who have been hurt or stripped of significance will always have a gap of loneliness. Loneliness is something that everyone battles and struggles with. It's the inner core of humanity, and it's the inner struggle of humanity that says, *I don't want to be alone*. It's the inner desire of humanity that cries out when no one else hears it crying out, pleading for someone to be close to. Loneliness is a fear that will grip your heart sooner or later in life; it's that place where humanity is afraid to go. Loneliness is a byproduct of intimacy.

It's okay to struggle with loneliness. We all do, but it's not okay to cave into loneliness. Once we cave into loneliness, there is a tendency to lose contact with everything. Why do we often feel alone and unloved? This book is about significance, and the less significant you feel, the lonelier you will feel.

If you are facing a time in your life when loneliness has settled in, know that it's something we all face. I would encourage you to read Psalm 42. It was written during a time when David thirsted for God. He was depressed and lonely. "As The deer pants for streams of water, so my soul pants for you, O God" (Psalm 42:1 NIV). Don't give up! "Let us not become weary in doing good, for at the proper time we will reap a harvest if we do not give up" (Gal. 6:9 NIV).

Opportunities arrives on the road of bumps and hurdles.

Opportunities don't come all at once! They come one step at a time and one day at a time! O

Seizing opportunities begins with taking care of the now opportunities, and the future opportunities will take care of themselves. "In their heart's humans plan their course, but the Lord determines his steps" (Prov. 16:9 NIV). Opportunities are hidden behind the bumps and hurdles of life. Just because there are bumps and hurdles does not mean that you have gotten off track along the road less traveled. Our next journey will be found through the bumps and hurdles, Therefore, since we are surrounded by such a great cloud of witnesses, let us throw off everything that hinders and the sin that so easily entangles. And Let us run with perseverance the race marked out for us. (Hebrews 12:1 NIV)

Not every opportunity is the right opportunity. *Opportunity* defined means, "Advantage, chance: A chance, especially one that offers advantage."

Opportunity is also defined as "Favorable conditions: A combination of favorable circumstances or situations."[11] "There is a time for everything, And a season for every activity under the heavens" (Eccl. 3:1 NIV). A time to cast away stones (old opportunities in the past that have been weighing you down); a time to gather new stones together (new opportunities, new creative thinking for those opportunities); a time to embrace and a time refrain from embracing (In each opportunity there will be an opportunity to refrain from embracing; that's where discernment comes in); a time to seek, and a time to lose (In life there will be times to seek out those new opportunities, and there will also be a time to lose those opportunities if we don't handle them properly, OUCH); a time to keep and a time to cast away (It's one thing to keep and hold onto those opportunities, but the true test will come when we have to cast away or give up those opportunities to receive new opportunities); a Time to *rend* (We can become so clingy and prideful in our opportunities that we forget that sometimes we have to tear it apart and rip apart in ways that will hurt us just to receive more opportunities); a time to *sew* (There is healing that comes with the opportunities that we willfully let go of and let God be. God wants to *sew* up every broken part that was being so prideful and so on); a time to keep silent (We don't have to talk about our opportunities; we can live out our opportunities by being silent and allowing what is right and true about our opportunities to speak for themselves.

A difficult road leads to the road of obedience.

One of the most inspirational people in the world, Mother Theresa, learned this road through Jesus's Sermon on the Mount, and she led by example and displayed it for many all over the world. A traveler on the road less traveled will always love their neighbor as themselves, Christian or non-Christian. It's a part of our DNA to be loved and to give love. One of the greatest principles and commandments in the Bible is to love our neighbor as ourselves. I must confess loving our neighbor as ourselves is something with which I struggle. I believe it's something we all struggle with at different times in our lives. That is why I believe the Sermon on the Mount is a key that we can use to unlock hidden things, to unlock the doors that have held people bound generation after generation.

Loving our neighbor as ourselves is the key that Mother Theresa used to touch the poor and the broken all over the world.

The Sermon on the Mount is something that everyone throughout history has put into practice at one point in their lives.

> 3 Blessed are the poor in spirit, for theirs is the kingdom of Heaven. 4 Blessed are those who mourn, for they will be comforted. 5 Blessed are the meek, for they will inherit the earth. 6 Blessed are those who hunger and thirst for righteousness, for they will be filled. 7 Blessed are the merciful, for they will be shown mercy. 8 Blessed are the pure in heart, for they will see God. 9 Blessed are the peacemakers, for they will be called children of God. 10 Blessed are those who are persecuted because of righteousness, for theirs is the kingdom of Heaven. (Matthew 5:3–10 NIV)

- Attitudes are everything; they affect everything we do, everything we say, and how we perceive things. Attitudes will be a determining factor in whether you lead a life above reproach (something I need to work on). Attitudes will also determine your level of success in life. If we constantly have the "we'll never amount to anything" attitude, then we can't succeed because we have bought into that attitude and become that attitude.

Let's look at the beatitudes through obedience.

In chapter 5 of Matthew's gospel we read, Matthew 5:3"Blessed are the poor in spirit, for theirs is the kingdom of Heaven." What does it mean to be poor in the spirit? Here is my viewpoint: Are we willing to give something up for others to have it? "Blessed" means happiness, so are we willing to go without during our difficult road? On the outside, we may not have much, but on the inside, we have much more. There are over 114 scriptures in the Bible that deal with taking care of the poor. We all call ourselves religious at one point or another. If we consider ourselves religious, are we displaying in our daily lives what it says in James 1: "Religion that God our Father accepts as pure and faultless is this: to look after orphans and widows in their distress and to keep oneself from being polluted by the world" (James 1:27 NIV). Can you imagine what would happen if each of us would help someone else in need every day, one person helping out one person every day? What would happen if we all took part in the effort to care for those in need?

Moving on to verse four, we find, "Blessed are those who mourn for they will be comforted." Obedience can lead to sorrow at first. There is always a price to be paid with obedience. Do we as a culture truly know what it is to mourn compared to countries that have experienced war or famine, where mourning has become part of everyday life? Take Haiti, for instance, a country that has faced devastation after devastation, famine after famine—don't get me wrong, I am completely aware of people who go through crises everyday who have mourned until they can mourn no more. My question is this, Have we mourned to the point of obedience that says yes to God no matter what I face; no matter what circumstance may come my way, It's easier said than done, but the Bible tells us to "Rejoice with those who rejoice, mourn with those who mourn" (Rom. 12:15 NIV). I believe if we would learn how to release our emotions the proper way, by mourning, we could see disease decrease. I believe if we would offer comfort to those who are mourning, we would see suicides decrease.

Now we reach the fifth verse: "Blessed are the meek for they will inherit the earth." (Blessed are the humble for they will inherit the earth.) In Peter's first letter, we read, "God resists the proud, but gives grace to the humble. 6 humble yourselves, under God's mighty hand, that he may lift you up in due time, 7 casting all your anxiety on him because he cares for you" (1Peter 5:6-7). Would you rather be known to God as a prideful or as a humble person?

A meek person is graceful and extends mercy. It's hard to extend mercy and grace when you have been wronged, so it speaks highly of your character when you extend grace and mercy when you have been wronged. We have all had those times when grace and mercy have been extended to us. My question is Can I do the same?

Verse six reads, "Blessed are those who hunger and thirst for righteousness for they shall be filled." Blessed are those who hunger and thirst for truth; blessed are those who live their lives above the typical standard of life. Are we satisfied with what we have and desire or is this deep hunger and thirst dwelling inside us to be expanded more for the right things.

The merciful are the focus of verse seven, "Blessed are the merciful for they will be shown mercy." We all need mercy at different times in our lives. Can we give mercy in the way we like to receive mercy? I know for me personally; it is easy for me hold grudges and not show mercy. At the same time, it's easy for me to want to receive mercy in the areas I mess up in. Receiving mercy can occur in different ways. "So, in everything, do to other's what you would have them do to you, for this sums up the Law and the Prophets. (Matthew7:12). Think about it, in any circumstance would you want to receive mercy?.

Verse eight tells us, "Blessed are the pure in heart for they will see God." Have you ever met individuals who are pure in heart who are always looking out for the best for other people, those who are constantly walking in humility, I believe this verse is talking about people like that. Even though they have their issues in life, they still walk out life with a positive outlook. Let's face it, we all have our "stuff" that troubles us. We all have our changes that we each realize we must make. Let me encourage you, "Create in me a pure heart, O God, and renew a steadfast spirit within me" (Psalm 51:10 NIV). "Above all else, guard your heart, for everything you do flows from it" (Prov. 4:23 NIV). The heart represents everything about a person; it is the central piece of every one of us.

Verse nine reads, "Blessed are the peacemakers for they will be called children of God." I think that one of the most difficult roads to travel is to offer peace and to bring peace. We see it every day in the news, and people experience it every day where their world is nothing but turmoil. Without peacemakers there will be chaos, disorder, confusion, uproar, mayhem, tumult, commotion, havoc, turbulence, unrest, and instability. I am sure there are words that hit home with you as you read this list because you have felt and experienced these types of conflict. "A gentle answer turns away wrath, but harsh words stir up anger. (Proverbs. 15:1 NIV). The way we express ourselves and conduct ourselves, what we say and how we say it, our body language can be what will bring either peace or discord. Controlling the way, we react to certain situations can cause a dismissal of chaos. Changing how we use words or refraining from lashing out in anger can reverse the direction of conflict, can bring disorder into order. I know I have a hard time controlling my tongue at times, so this is a road I need to work on personally. Thinking before reacting is another key area to becoming a peacemaker. How much confusion do we cause every day by speaking before we think or reacting before we think?

The last beatitude in Matthew5:10 Blessed are those who are persecuted because of righteousness, for theirs is the kingdom of heaven. Let's look at three areas where we all face persecution, whether we are Christian or non-Christian.

1: **Standing up for what you believe in**: Every time someone takes a stand for what they believe in, it is an indication that they will become a direct target in one form or another. Everyone has something they believe in, but only a few stand up for their beliefs.

2: **Being a dreamer:** Stepping outside of the box and daring to accomplish things no one else has ever achieved, believing something against all odds is dreaming. Everybody has a dream at one point or another in their lifetime. The key is to never give up on that dream, but not everybody chooses to travel the road to achieve that dream.

3: **Taking a stand for moral values; choosing not to listen to the voices of peer pressure.** We need people to take a stand for moral values and to denounce the voices of peer pressure that have caused our generation to cave in. Today it seems that almost an entire generation has been lost to a culture that has rejected the traditional moral values that built our society. We need voices to speak up for biblical values.

Types of Persecution Faced When Taking a Stand

1: **Standing up for what we believe in:** One of my favorite scriptures in the Bible is about David and Goliath. When you stand up for what you believe in, many giants will come your way to try to stifle your beliefs. David, however, stood his ground and believed God. Look at David's response in First Samuel when Goliath tried to stifle what David believed in, "David asked the men standing near him, "What will be done for the man who kills this Philistine and removes this disgrace from Israel? Who is this uncircumcised Philistine that he should defy the armies of the living God?" (1 Samuel. 17:26 NIV). When you stand up for what you believe in and take a stand for Christ, no persecution can stifle you. When we face persecution, may God give us the same solid belief in his presence and the commitment to our faith that David exhibited. Let's pray for the same perspective that David had, and let's stand up during persecution. In First Samuel 17:45, David said to the Philistine, "You come against me with sword and spear and javelin, but I come against you in the name of the Lord Almighty, the God of the Armies of Israel whom you have defied." God will fight your battles for you as you stand up for him. We need to be like David in standing up for what we believe in. David was *defiant* against Goliath. You see, for David the key that unlocked the door was he stood up for what was right. The same is true for you. When you stand up for what is right, God will give you a defiant edge as he did for David against those who dare to persuade you.

2: Being a Dreamer. People will try to steal your dream; people will bombard you with negative stuff. They'll say your dream will never come true. Let's look at some dreamers in the Bible. It's not the big voices that will kill a dream, it's the little, small voices that will paralyze a dream. The small dream killer voices that we often listen to will often turn into larger voices if we allow them to. Joseph understood what it was to be a dreamer. He also understood what is to see your dream persecuted. If your dream has been persecuted in any way, I would encourage you to read the story of Joseph's life beginning in Genesis 37:1 and ending at Genesis 50:26. God may very well use persecution not to kill your dream but only to make your dream stronger. You intended to harm me, but God intended it for good to accomplish what is now being done, the saving of many lives. (Genesis. 50:20 NIV). God can bring something good out of the worst-case circumstances during persecution. The bigger the dream is, the larger the battle is. The more you put into your dream, the more people will put into seeing your dream fulfilled. When chasing your dream, allow the wind of the Spirit to be on your back to propel you to your destiny. When the walls of your dreams seem to be crumbling around you, allow God himself to remold and rebuild those crumbling walls. Only a few people know this, but I have had a dream tucked away in my heart for about thirteen years, and that is the dream of seeing my family completely restored. I believe with all my heart, with every ounce that I have in me that God has given me that promise, and it will come to pass—not in my timing but in his—and the generational curses shall be broken, the prison chains shall be broken, and my family shall walk free. "But if serving the Lord seems undesirable to you, then choose for yourselves this day whom you will serve, whether the Gods your ancestors served beyond the Euphrates, or the gods of the Amorites, in whose land you are living. But as for me and my household, [family] we will serve the Lord" (Joshua 24:15 NIV).

What about you? What is your dream in this journey? What road less traveled are you willing to travel to see that dream fulfilled.

3: **Taking a Stand for Moral Values.** It's our choice whether to take a stand for moral values. It's a choice that is set before us every day. It's a choice that I have often failed to stand for.

> 15 See, I set before you today life and prosperity, death, and destruction. 16 For I command you today to love the Lord your God, to walk in obedience to him, and to keep his commands, decrees, and laws; then you will live and increase, and the Lord your God will bless you in the land you are entering to possess. (Deuteronomy 30:15–16 NIV)

The Bible is clear, if we take a stand for moral values, God will bless us. Keeping his commands is standing up for moral values. God wants us to live a life that is fulfilled, if we are fulfilled in him and through him. As we are keeping his commands, the moral values we must keep are found in the ten commandments, which comprise the moral values that we must take a stand for. If we don't, then we will lose the battle we face every day.

The more significant you are the more vulnerable you are.

People who influence the way we live our lives rise and fall every day. If you don't believe me, all you must do is watch the news and see it happening for yourself. My question to that is this: Why is it the more significant you are the more vulnerable you are? Let's take another look at the ten commandments and see.

1: Matthew 4:10 NIV—Jesus said to him " Away from me, Satan! For it is written: 'Worship the Lord your God and Serve Him Only.

When we are at the bottom, it's easy to look to God for everything and anything in life. When you're significant and have influence, it's easy to get all tripped out on yourself and take your focus off him and instead focus on yourself by thinking that you can get away with anything and everything by your significance and influence. Every day we see those we idolize, those we look up to, forget who made them and become more by the enticement of saying I can get away with it.

2: "No servant can serve both masters" (Luke 16:13 NIV). Have you ever noticed when we are elevated into a higher position how easy it is to be in way over our heads about the situation and go overboard with the position? I know I do, and when I come to those points, I must recognize within myself that I am serving more than one master.

3: "You shall not misuse the name of the Lord your God" (Exodus. 20:7 NIV). The public eye is constantly on those who make a difference. Our friends' and family's eyes are constantly on us when we take a stand for something. Every word that comes from our lips either speaks life or death into the individuals whose lives we encounter every day. It's so easy for us to misuse words, allowing people to take what we say and turn it into something negative if we are not careful in our approach to what we say.

4: "Remember the Sabbath Day by keeping it holy. (Exodus. 20:8 NIV) It is so easy to end up getting burned out by not taking care of us and by not resting. The Sabbath was created for one purpose— for us to rest. How often do we get so caught up in doing what it is that we do that we end up getting fatigued and burned out and don't take out time to rest. In having influence and significance in life, there must be a balance of also having rest, having a day off. I believe one of the crucial fault lines in families that has been broken is in the requirement of resting and spending time with each other.

5: "Honor your father and your mother, so that you may live long in the land the Lord your God is giving you" (Exodus. 20:12 NIV). For many, this will be hard because of the separation that thousands of families have faced; it's still something I struggle with every day, and something I am trying to teach myself to do every day. I believe family is the puzzle piece to humanity. If you take away the middle part of a puzzle, the puzzle will never be shaped to its completed form. The same is true with our families. The middle piece, the family's core values and the family itself, have been missing and we don't know what true family looks like anymore.

6: "But I tell you that Anyone who is angry with his brother will be subject to judgement. (Matthew. 5:22 NIV). People hold grudges. It's easy for me to hold a grudge, but it's more difficult for me to let go of a grudge. We as a church, as America, and as individuals have become vulnerable by allowing ourselves to become angry that it's literally consuming us every day. If we harbor things, there will be consequences such as health issues, depression, and so many other things. Short fuses can often turn into explosions if we do not learn to control our anger.

7: "But I tell you that Anyone who looks at a woman lustfully has already committed adultery with her in his heart. (Matthew. 5:28 NIV). This is the number one area where all guys are weak; it's a weakness that has taken out men of significance and influence throughout history. It has also taken out men of God. Men, let's be honest with ourselves: when we look at a woman with lustful intentions, we are already picturing what we are doing in our minds. Looking at girls with the wrong intentions is a major struggle of mine. Yet, I want the woman of God to come into my life when I can't even control my own lust. We need men of chivalry to rise and ask God to guard our eyes, our hearts, and our thought patterns against this attack.

Men of Chivalry

Men of chivalry have a combination of qualities, especially courage, honor, loyalty, and consideration for others. especially women I long to be is a man of chivalry. Let's look at two different people in the Bible who were faced with lust and see how the two reacted and compare how they responded.

> 11 One day he went into the house to attend to his duties, and none of the household servants was inside. 12 She caught him by his cloak and said, "Come to bed with me!' But he left his cloak in her hand and ran out of the house. (Genesis. 39:11–12 NIV). It takes a *man* to respond the way Joseph did; "he left his cloak in her hand and ran out of the house."

> 2 One evening David got up from his bed and walked around on the roof of the palace. From the roof he saw a woman bathing. The woman was very beautiful, 3 and David sent someone to find out about her. The man said, "She is Bathsheba, the daughter of Eliam and the wife of Uriah the Hittite." 4 Then David sent messengers to get her. She came to him, and he slept

> with her. (Now she was purifying herself from her monthly uncleanness.) Then she went back home. 5 The woman conceived and sent the word to David, saying, "I am pregnant." (2 Samuel 11:2–5 NIV)

The difference between the two men, between Joseph and David, is that Joseph was able to run from his lust when he had a chance. David fell into the trap of his lust. I will be the first to admit I have fallen into many traps of lust. There will always be an opportunity to run from our lust if we choose to run and flee.

8   "And If anyone wants to sue you and take your shirt, hand over your coat as well" (Matt. 5:40 NIV). It's hard to find generous people; it's so easy to get caught up in what is in it for us that we lose sight for what is in it for other people by being generous.

9   "But I tell you that everyone will have to give account on the day of judgment for every empty word they have spoken" (Matt. 12:36 NIV). Men, you'll have to give account for every careless word that you have spoken. One word from us can either be life or death to someone, and we will have to give account for our words. I cannot even begin to tell you how words have shaped my life

and shaped the way I viewed myself. I believe confidence, self-esteem, and worth are often shaped by the words that are spoken over us.

10 "Then he said to them, 'Watch out! Be on your guard against all kinds of greed; life does not consist in an abundance of possessions" (Luke 12:15 NIV). Successful people can be greedy people.

Significant people can be greedy people; people of influence can be greedy people. Greed is evident all around us. It seems the more we have the more we want. We all face it every day; that's why we must be on our guard against it every day.

a vision for someone's life is often not seen in the small picture of what they are looking at into the future, but in the bigger picture into the future of their life, I Believe God wants to show each of you that are reading this book the bigger picture of your Journey to Significane.

Ways we get caught up in the drift of seeing the smaller picture.

Worry: Developing a mindset that tells us we will never break out of the cycle, and out of the box, and only being able to see what is in front of us, and not what beyond us is worrying. We can become so bombarded by worry that it can cause us to lose focus on the bigger picture of life, leaving us focusing on the smaller picture only.

One of my favorite scriptures dealing with the seeing the bigger picture of our lives is found in Philippians. These two verses will help us quit seeing the smaller picture of our life.

> Brothers and sisters, I do not consider myself yet to have taken a hold of it. [Time-out: Paul is talking about obtaining the bigger picture of his life instead of obtaining the smaller picture of his life] But one thing I do: Forgetting what is behind me [the smaller picture of our life] and straining toward what is ahead, [the bigger picture; also, Paul is saying "I push and I strain every day to see the bigger picture of my life fulfilled. Unless we push and strain and fight, we will never see the bigger picture of our life and will always be stuck in the smaller picture of our life] I press on toward the goal to win the prize for which God has called me heavenward in Christ Jesus [the bigger picture]. (Phil. 3:13–14 NIV, emphasis added)

Why does everything bad have to happen to me? That's an outlook I often have in life, and it's an outlook I am trying to walk out. That outlook can cause us to look at the smaller picture of our life instead of the larger picture of our life. I am absolutely inspired by people who come from the worst situations of life and turn their lives around and make them into the best-case situations. We can either stay in our self-pity, and keep looking at the smaller picture of our life while wishing for something else, or we can take a stand and say, "You know what, my situations and circumstances may suck, but I will not allow them to hold us prisoner any longer, in the name of Jesus let's see those chains of that mindset, those chains of self-pity, broken. I remember when someone who has spoken into my life told me to let God be God.

Now I say those words to you: Let God be God and you be you and rise above of this situation and circumstance.

On viewing the smaller picture, the Bible says, "See I am doing a new thing! Now it springs up; do you not perceive it? I am making a way in the wilderness and streams in the wasteland" (Isa. 43:19 NIV). God wants to do a new thing. No longer view your life as something bad, instead, view your life as something good.

On Thinking That You Can't See the Bigger Picture

If you shift your mind into the right, you will always be able to look past the small pictures and see the bigger picture of your life. When life seems to be spinning out of control and all you can see is the small picture, remind yourself of who you are, not who others say you are. You can accomplish something great, but you can't accomplish the bigger picture of your life without first thinking that you can.

The bigger picture of your life is your journey. When you see it, you find yourself. Can I share a secret with you? He knows the bigger picture of your life and is waiting to reveal it you. It's your own to walk out in this life. No one else has your picture of life—only you can be the unique you—go and discover the bigger picture of your life. "Now to him who is able to do immeasurably more than all we ask or imagine, according to his power that is at work within us" (Eph. 3:20 NIV).

Go Forward this day in everything God has for you to walk in his ways.

Walk in Truth.

Walk in Hope.

Walk in Joy.

Walk in Peace.

Walk now as God has created you to walk. Travel on the road less traveled to change our world around us as sons and daughters of the King of Kings.

5

Significance Begins from the Bottom Up

As we go through this final chapter together, let us look at three Different Men of God in the Bible: Joseph, Jeremiah, and David.

From the Pit to the Palace

There was a long period in my life where I always had this view of being in the pit instead of in the palace I would beat myself up time and time again over failures, mistakes, and so many other things that I reached the point in life where I was living a life in the pit instead of living a life in the palace. Often God will use the pits of life to propel us to the palace of our life. I have often struggled to understand the pits of life. The pit of insignificance, especially, has been a tremendous downfall for me. Feeling insignificant has crippled me to the point where everything I did, I felt like I'd failed. I will never forget how my masters commission family stood up for me and stood with me during the times I felt like I couldn't do anything or accomplish anything.

Joseph's life is the perfect example of how we need to trust God through the pits so we can get to the palaces of life. Joseph learned early on in life that significance is not found on the mountaintops, the summits of life. Significance is found in the lowest points in life. It's the lowest points in life that build our foundation in significance for the summits of life. Joseph's life was built for significance through the pits he was in. Your significance, too, will not be seen in the highest peaks of life. True significance is seen in the lowest pits of life.

Joseph lived through four stages of the pit.

Stage One: Being Sold by His Own Family all for a Dream.

"Here Comes that, Dreamer!" They said to each other. Come now, let's kill him and throw him into one of these cisterns and say that a ferocious animal devoured him. Then we'll see what comes of his dreams" (Gen. 37:19–20 NIV). Before Joseph could ever be trusted to lead a whole nation, he had to be trusted to lead his own life from the pit to the palace. Can you imagine what was going through Joseph's own mind when he was sold? They hid him in an empty, isolated cistern. In our own isolations of life, our cisterns, do we view ourselves as significant or insignificant? Joseph understood the ladder of success.

Joseph understood that everything in life is not built from the top up but only from the bottom up.

Stage 2: Prisons

Joseph's master took him and put him in prison, the place where the king's prisoners were confined. But while Joseph was there in prison, the Lord was with him; he showed him kindness and granted him favor in the eyes of the prison warden" (Gen. 39:20–21 NIV). Check this out: "Joseph could have seen his situation as hopeless, instead he did his best with each *small* task given to him."[12] I believe there were specific reasons why God allowed Joseph to be placed in prison. There were certain lessons to be learned before he could be put in charge of anything. There were certain characteristics that needed to be cut off for the new characteristics to be put on. When stuff doesn't go the way we planned, When the circumstances get too tense, how often do we bicker and complain instead of doing what Joseph did, which is accept this season of life as a kingdom teacher to better ourselves for the bigger things that God has planned for us by taking care of foundational things of life?

Stage 3: Dying to the Right to Say I Have the Right to Hold On

6 Now Joseph was the governor of the land, the person who sold grain to all its people. So when Joseph's brothers

arrived, they bowed down to him with their faces to the ground. 7 As soon as Joseph saw his brothers, he recognized them, but he pretended to be a stranger and spoke harshly to them. "Where do you come from?"he asked. 'From the Land of Canaan,' they replied, 'to buy food" (Gen. 42:6–7 NIV).

Joseph had every right to be angry, bitter, unforgiving, broken, and so many other things, against his brothers, but Joseph didn't have the right to hold on to his anger if he wanted to be built up from the bottom up.. I believe this type of stuff happens every day, no matter who you are. Where something bad happens and we give ourselves the excuse that we have the right to hold onto our hurt, to carry it, to nurture it, and to birth it. If you look at it, that's what we do every day. We have given ourselves the right to feel that way, so it's no wonder it's so easy to become bitter, angry, unforgiving, and so on. Then we all wonder why we are not moving forward to the next stage. We will remain in every stage of life until we pass it. We can't run from it, we can't hide from it, and we can't escape it. So why not pass it like Joseph did and move on through the strength, mercy, and grace of God in your life.

Stage 4: Seeing Through God's Rearview Mirror and Not Our Own Mirror of the Past

> 1 Then Joseph could no longer control himself before all his attendants, and he cried out "Have everyone leave my

presence! So that there was no one with Joseph when he made himself known to his brothers. 2 And he wept so loudly that the Egyptians heard him, and Pharaoh's household heard about it. 3 Joseph said to his brothers, "I am Joseph! Is my father still living?" But his brothers were not able to answer him, because they were terrified at his presence (Genesis 45:1–3 NIV).

The birthing pains that Joseph went through for years finally ceased. Has there ever been a time in your life where something has happened or when you were released from something and the emotions of the moment were uncontrollable. I believe that's how Joseph felt in verse 1. God wants to take me and you from the place of birthing pains to the place of birth where you can finally say, "I have the right to claim my birthright." Through all the pain, through all the despair, through all the heartache, we can come to the place where we are no longer confined to our birthing pains but to the place to where we are released to our birthright through passing the stages that lead up to seeing our own past through God's rearview mirror and not the mirror of our past. Joseph could have used his brothers' fear to his advantage but chose not to do so. The final choice to see through God's rearview mirror and not our own, is our choice, and God will always empower us to make the right choice if we choose to.

Then Joseph said to his brothers, "Come close to me." When they had done so, he said, "I am your brother Joseph, the one you sold into Egypt," 5 And now, do not be distressed and do not be angry with yourselves for selling me here, because it was to save lives that God sent me ahead of you. 6 For two years now there has been famine in the land, and for the next five years there will be no plowing and reaping. 7 But God sent me ahead of you to preserve for you a remnant on earth and to save your lives by a great deliverance. (Gen. 45:4–7 NIV)

Time out: If I was Joseph, when his brothers got close to him, I would have smacked them until they turned purple. Thank God I am not Joseph, though, and we all say, "Amen." Joseph learned something, a lesson that maturity and character is developed from the bottom up. If we were in Joseph's shoes in those moments, would we have been able to respond in the way that Joseph responded? Significance is developed through maturity and character. God will never trust us to carry the birthrights until we have the maturity and character to carry the birthing pains. We need to understand that, through God's lens, everything begins on the inside of us not on the outside of us.

When you don't understand why certain things happen, why certain circumstances unfold, look at like this, God sent you ahead of the circumstances to prepare you to help lead others out of those same circumstances. God will never waste your pain. The pain you carry is your birthright to see birthed into something that will lead others out of the same pain and heartache.

So then it was not you who sent me here, but God. He made me father to Pharaoh, lord of his entire household and ruler of all Egypt. Now hurry back to my father and say to him. "This is what your son says, God has made me Lord of all Egypt. Come to me don't delay. You shall live near the region of Goshen and be near me—you, your children and your grandchildren, your flocks, and herds, and all you have. I will provide for you there, because five years of famine are still to come. Otherwise, you and your household and all who belong to you will become destitute." (Gen. 45:8–12 NIV)

God has a plan no matter where you are in life. God has a purpose for your life. No matter where you find yourself, God's love for you is stretched out this day to pick you up and to take you from the place where you are to the place to where you are going. The same thing he did for Joseph and his family, he will do for you.

> You can see for yourselves, and so can my brother Benjamin, that it is really I who am speaking to you. 13 Tell

my father about all the honor accorded me in Egypt and about everything you have seen. And bring my father down here quickly." 14 Then he threw his arms around his brother Benjamin and wept, and Benjamin embraced him, weeping, 15 and he kissed all his brothers and wept over them. Afterward his brothers talked with him (Gen. 45:12–15 NIV).

The key to Joseph's success relates to what God was doing on the inside of him; through that, it produced many things on the outside of him. How often is God trying to change us, and we are fighting against him, unwilling to go through the process and never arrive to the place of our birthrights? We all need kingdom God to work within our hearts in order to arrive at the place of birthrights. Each stage we face in life is another preparation for reaching everything God has for us.

Like Joseph, we have all been commissioned to go forward, to allow the Holy Spirit to build our foundation from the bottom up before our next journey. Let's take another look at someone God had to build from the bottom up.

Peter: Thinking we have gone above our foundation

"But Peter declared, 'Even if I have to die with you, I will never disown you,' And all the other disciples said the same" (Matt. 26:35 NIV)

Peter made the mistake that I believe we all make—running ahead of something before it is ever built. Has there been a time where something has come up, and the thought ran through your head that you would never do the same thing? I don't know about you, but I've had that happen many times when I acted on impulse before ever thinking about my actions because of an unstable foundation. Every foundation has a weak part to it that in an instant can crumble if we try to build prematurely on our foundation before it is complete.

In these next several verses we will see Peter becoming something that he never thought he would become. We will see Peter acting on a thought that he promised he would never act on. If we are not careful and wait for the proper foundation to be built, it's so easy to become something that we told ourselves we would never become.

> Now Peter was sitting in the courtyard, and a servant girl came to him. "You also were with Jesus of Galilee," she said. But he denied it before them all. "I don't know what you're talking about," he said. Then he went out to the gateway, where another

girl saw him and said to the people there. "This fellow was with Jesus of Nazareth." He denied it again with an oath. "I don't know the man." After a little while, those standing there went up to Peter and said, "Surely you are one of them; for your accent gives you away." Then he began to call down curses on himself and he swore to them. "I don't know the man!" Immediately, a rooster crowed. Then Peter remembered the word Jesus had spoken: "Before the rooster crows you will disown me three times." And he went outside and wept bitterly. (Matthew 26:69–75 NIV)

Do you see? There are many different reasons why we do the same things that we say we will never do.

Training Camp

To stay in alignment with our foundation, we must train ourselves every day on what to do and what not to do, on what to say and what not to say, on how to act and how to react to anything that comes our way. I believe Peter meant what he said when he said to Jesus that he would never disown him, but Jesus saw something that Peter didn't see. Jesus saw a faulty foundation with missing pieces. He saw that Peter needed to walk the route he needed to walk.

Training Camp: Controlling what comes out of your mouth.

"Likewise, the tongue is a small part of the body, but it makes great boasts. Consider what a great forest is set on fire by a small spark" (James 3:5 NIV). Have you ever heard of the phrase "think before you speak"? If anyone does, I should be the one having that stamped on my forehead, so I can see it every day. Peter made the mistake that we all make. He spoke something before he thought about it. Peter may have had the right intentions for what he said, but he didn't back up those right intentions. When I get frustrated and angry and so on, that's when it becomes easy for me to have uncontrolled speech that leads to one thing after another, and there it's easy to fall through the cracks of a faulty foundation. Peter's words were a small spark that led to a huge fire. Through the "Training Camp" of speech control, Jesus revealed a greater portion of who Peter could become. We should always train our speech every day, in order to become who we are to become in God's plan.

Boot Camp: Like you and me, Peter had a lesson to learn. Peter needed to not get ahead of himself and be somewhere that he was not yet ready to be.

"I'm going out to fish," Simon Peter told them, and they said, "We'll go with you." So, they went out and got into the boat, but that night they caught nothing" (John 21:3 NIV). Here, Peter was being commissioned by the Lord as a rock for the kingdom, and now he's back to being rubble. The enemy would like nothing more than to steal the treasured times that the Lord has called for in your life and pervert them into something to see you left to become nothing but rubble. Peter was back to the same thing, not being able to catch anything. How often does that happen with us? How often do we say we won't do something we have promised ourselves we wouldn't do and end up doing it and then making an excuse to get out of it? When we fail at something, and try to overcome it, and keep on failing at it, it's like Boot Camp. You got to keep getting back up; you got to keep reminding yourself that you can overcome and not be held down by the mistakes.

Come on and rise, for I have not forgotten about you; Jesus, the great I am, sees us in our journey and promises to never forsake us. Just as he did for Peter, I will do for you. Rise up, walk, be freed, continue your journey, and allow me to weave you into the womb of my kingdom, to be built from the bottom up. Love God. Like a boxing match, you got a ten count. Let God give you the strength and freedom to get back up and continue onward and upward in your journey to significance.

A Full Recovery

"But go, tell his disciples and Peter, 'He is going ahead of you into Galilee. There you will see him, just as he told you" (Mark 16:7 NIV). God has not forgotten you or left you in insignificance; God has a *full recovery* in store you. In your worst days, in the days where all hell seems to break out, in the times it seems like life has laid you out, Jesus is around the corner saying *My Son and Daughter, I have gone before you and ahead of you. I have not left you or abandoned you. I am here. Just as my angel sent out the message that I was going ahead of my disciples and Peter, so I send you this message. I am here right now ready give you a full recovery.*

Can you imagine what was going through Peter's mind? His thought process probably went something like this, *Man, Peter, you really screwed this one up. Man, Peter, how many times are you going to mess up opportunities to be accepted. Man, Peter, why can't you at least do one thing right with your life? Man, Peter, there is no hope, for you have been given chance after chance.*

I don't know about you, but I have had those thoughts appear in my head time and time again; that continually affects the outlook I have on my inward and outward life.

5 He called out to them, "Friends, haven't you any fish?" "No," they answered. 6 He said, "Throw your net on the right side of the boat and you will find some." When they did, they were unable to haul the net in because of

123

the large number of fish. 7 Then the disciple who Jesus loved said to Peter, "It is the Lord!" As soon as Simon Peter heard him say, "It is the Lord," he wrapped his outer garment around him, for he had taken it off) and jumped into the water. 8 The other disciples followed in the boat, towing the net full of fish, for they were not far from shore, about a hundred yards. 9 When they landed, they saw a fire of burning coals there with fish on it, and some bread 10 Jesus said to them, "Bring some of the fish you just have caught."11 So Simon Peter climbed aboard and dragged the net ashore. It was full of large fish, but even with so many the net was not torn" (John 21:5–11 NIV).

Notice both scenes with Peter involved water. Each scene required Peter to step out beyond what he had known, into something greater that he was getting ready to know. Keep this scripture in mind.

27 But Jesus immediately said them: "Take courage! It is I. Don't be afraid." 28 "Lord, if it's you," Peter replied, "tell me to come to you on the water." 29 "Come," he said. Then Peter got down out of the boat, walked on the water, and came toward Jesus. 30 But when he saw the wind, he was afraid, and, beginning to sink, cried out, "Lord, Save me!" 31 Immediately, Jesus reached out his hand and caught him, "You of little faith," he said, "why did you doubt?" 32 And when they climbed into the boat, the wind died down. (Matthew 14:27–32 NIV)

Scene 1 Peter's heart began to leap within him because in that moment he realized that life wasn't over for him; Matthew 14:27 Jesus said Take courage It is I. In that moment Peter realized that his failure didn't dictate his future in everything that God had designed for him, every time we are given a second chance to live a life of significance, something begins to leap within us Something begins to stir within us. God can turn your greatest mistakes, into your greatest success stories. Did you notice in Matthew 14:30 as soon as Peter cried out Lord save me! The savior reached down and cause him and saved him. In our mistakes Jesus is there to catch us and immediately pull us back up. Peter had this understanding that none of the other disciples had. He understood that Jesus didn't forget about him, and that Jesus didn't give up on him. It's so easy to forget about what Jesus has done and will continue do. Peter must have kept something tucked deep in his heart that suddenly began to stir when the King of Kings was calling his name. At one point in Matthew we read, "And I tell you that you are Peter, and on this rock, I will build my church and the gates of Hades will not overcome it" (Matt. 16:18 NIV). When life sucks and everything seems lost, remember something he has promised you. Some reading this may say, "Daniel, I have never heard his voice. Daniel, I don't know who this Jesus is. Daniel, the mess has covered up everything that I held onto and can no longer see it, believe it, or hear it." If so, then begin to pronounce blessings over yourself instead of denouncing negative stuff over yourself. Let me help you bless yourself.

Heaven has an announcement designed specifically for you, to denounce everything that hell says.

4 Rejoice in the Lord always! I will say it again: Rejoice! 5 Let your gentleness be evident to all. The Lord is near. 6 Do not be anxious about anything, but in every situation, by prayer and petition, with thanksgiving, present your request to God. 7 And the peace of God which transcends all understanding, will guard your hearts and minds in Christ Jesus. 8 Finally, brothers and sisters, whatever is true, whatever is noble, whatever is right, whatever is pure, whatever is lovely, whatever is admirable—if anything is excellent or praiseworthy—think about such things. 9Whatever you have learned or received or heard from me, or seen in me—put it into practice. And the God of peace will be with you (Philippians 4:4–9 NIV)

Peter was desperate to see the Lord, in fact, he was so desperate that he may have said something like this to the other disciples. "I don't know about you, but as for me, I am head over heels for my Lord. As for me, I messed up and he is still calling me. As for me, I don't want to live a comfortable life in the boat of religion. I am jumping over and swimming directly to him.

Scene 2

Jesus comes walking along seas of significance into the stormy seashores of insignificance. The Message version puts it this way.

> But Jesus was quick to comfort them. "Courage, it's me. don't be afraid. Peter, suddenly bold, said "Master if it's really you, call me to you on the water. He said, "Come ahead." Jumping out of the boat, Peter walked on the water to Jesus. but when he looked down at the waves churning beneath his feet, he lost his nerve and started to sink. He cried, "Master Save Me!" Jesus didn't hesitate. he reached down and grabbed his hand. Then he said, "Faint-heart, What Got into you? The two of them climbed into the boat, and the wind died down. The Disciples in the boat having watched the whole thing, worshiped Jesus, saying, "This is it! you are God's son for sure!" (Matthew 14:27–33 MSG)

Notice that Jesus was quick to comfort them, "Courage, it is me don't be afraid." In that moment, all alone in the stormy seashores of insignificance, I can't help but think how helpless the disciples must have felt in the middle of the storm. Isn't that what insignificance does to us? It makes feel helpless, it leaves us feeling like *This is it for me*; *This is the end of the road for me*. If we can just look past the storms of insignificance and see the sea of significance that Jesus is walking on toward our insignificance, we could also hear his voice, "Have I not commanded you? Be strong and of great courage! Do not be afraid; do not be discouraged, for the Lord your God will be with you wherever you go" (Josh. 1:9 NIV). Don't be alarmed by these storms! For I have great significance that I want to reveal to you through the calm seashores that I take you by the hand and walk with you through every season of Life.

Peter, suddenly bold said, "Master, if it's really you, call me to you on the water. (Matthew 14:28 The Message) Have you ever heard the saying, "Watch what you wish for"? Peter was saying this, "Lord. help me to walk away from my insignificance into your significance. Has it ever happened to you that from out of nowhere you had this sudden burst of boldness to do something that you wouldn't normally do? I believe that's what we need—a burst of Holy Ghost boldness to walk out of our insignificance into our true dominion, into being people significance. Once we start toward our significance, we can never look back at our insignificance. But how often do we do that? We look back. Luke says, "Jesus replied, "No one who puts his hands to the plow and looks for back is

fit for service in the kingdom of God" (Luke 9:62 NIV).
The reason it says that is because if we look back this is
what will happen, and it happens to all of us.

29-30 He said, 'Come ahead.' Jumping out of the
boat, Peter walked on the water to Jesus. But when he
looked down at the waves churning beneath his feet, he
lost his nerve and started to sink. He cried, Master, save
me!" (Matthew. 14:29–30 MSG). How many can be with
honest with themselves and evaluate the times when we
were walking on calm seas of life when a storm suddenly
appeared, and we looked downward at the storm instead
of upward? In those moments all we could see was our
insignificance—how defenseless we were in those situations—and we began to sink again because we looked
back or looked down at our insignificance. We began to
sink deeper and deeper until we could no longer hold
onto our significance. If that's you, the most significant
thing that you can do in your life is say what Peter said,
"Master Save me! Master Save me, In Jesus's name.

"Jesus didn't hesitate, he reached down and grabbed
his hand. Then he said, 'Faint-heart, what got into you?'
The two of them climbed into the boat, and the wind died
down. The disciples in the boat having watched the whole
thing, worshiped Jesus, saying, 'This is it! *You are God's
Son for sure!*'" (Matt. 14:31–33 MSG, emphasis added). At
the sound of your voice saying, "Master, Save me!" God
will never hesitate to pick you up from where you are in

the storms of life and bring you into the place that you were always meant to be, and that's with him.

Appointment

There he went into the cave and spent the night. and the word of the Lord came to him

"What are you doing here, Elijah? 10 He replied, "I have been very zealous for the Lord God almighty. the Israelites have rejected your covenant, torn down your altars, and put your prophets to death with the sword. I am the only one left, and now they are trying to kill me too. 11 The Lord said, "Go out and stand on the mountain in the presence of the Lord, for the Lord is about to pass by." Then a great and powerful wind tore the mountains apart and shattered the rocks before the Lord. but the Lord was not in the wind. After the wind there was an earthquake, but the Lord was not in the earthquake. 12 After the earthquake came a fire. but the lord was not in the fire. and after the fire came a gentle whisper. 13vWhen Elijah heard it, he pulled his cloak over his face and went out and stood at the mouth of the cave. Then a voice said to him "What are you doing here Elijah?" (1 Kings 19:9–13)

In verse 9 above, Elijah went into the cave and spent the night, and the word of the Lord came to him, "What are you doing here Elijah?" But let's go back a couple of verses and see the reason why Elijah spent the night in the cave. In 1 Kings 19 we read:

1 Now Ahab told Jezebel everything Elijah had done and how he had killed all the prophets with the sword. 2 So Jezebel sent a messenger to Elijah to say "may the Gods deal with me be it ever so severely, if by this time tomorrow I do not make your life like that of one of them." 3 Elijah was afraid and ran for his life. When he came to Beersheba in Judah, he left his servant there. (1 Kings 19:1–3)

In 1 Kings 18 God used Elijah in a significant event, and in chapter 19 we see Elijah running for his life. Every time something significant happens in your life, have you noticed how something will try to destroy those significant moments? After we find something significant about us, something will happen that will cause us to feel less significant. Like Elijah, we need to run to shelter when those moments come and find ourselves again in him. When discouragement settles in revert it with encouragement.

Then, let's re-read this section,

The Lord said "go out and stand on the mountain in the presence of the Lord, for the Lord is about to pass by. Then a great and powerful wind tore the mountains apart and shattered the rocks before the

> Lord *But the Lord was not in the wind.* after the wind there *was an earthquake. But the Lord was not in the earthquake either. After the earthquake came a fire, but the Lord was not in the fire either. And after the fire, came a gentle whisper. When Elijah heard it, he pulled his cloak over his face and went out and stood at the mouth of the cave. Then a voice said to him, "What are you doing here Elijah?"*

Just as in Elijah's situation, significance is never found in the big things in life. Significance is always found by individuals who are willing to be built from bottom up. Like Elijah, could it be that we are looking for something big when what we should be looking for is a gentle whisper, is a gentle question, asking us, "What are you doing here?"

Wind

Wind represents the moments in life where everything in life has been turned upside down and thrown against the wall of confusion. Elijah had to see for himself that God was still in control. Even though Elijah was no longer in control of his life, he had to still see that God was still in control. Elijah had just defeated the false prophets through the fire and God, and now Elijah was running for his life. Talk about the wind of confusion!

I remember a time when the wind of confusion swept me away. I didn't know what I was doing, I Didn't know where I was going in life. The wind of confusion can be seen in anyone's life, especially seniors in high school and college students because it's around that time when major decisions have to be made about the future. And a lot of times, these decisions leave us confused about what to do. In times of confusion, listen for the gentle whisper telling you what to do. Build from the bottom up so that when the wind does come, you will have a firm foundation. The wind of confusion can toss us and turn us upside down if our foundation is not well built. Never look at the other windstorms of peoples' lives because that will continue to bring in even more confusion.

Earthquake

No matter how strong something is, an earthquake will always cause something to crumble and collapse. The earthquakes of life's oppositions and oppressions can only affect the outward things, not the inward things. When lust comes into a man's life, if he has not guarded his heart and disciplined himself to turn away and look the other direction, the earthquake causes everything to collapse. Men, do you realize how significant that would be in your girlfriend's eyes or your wife's eyes, if you could say that you turned away and are standing. Ladies, when the earthquake of culture says how to dress, how to look, and how to act comes in, you realize how significant it is when you say, *I will not put my body through that and I refuse to show my body off*. What about the earthquake anger? "An angry man stirs up conflict and a hot-tempered one commits many sins. (Prov. 29:22 NIV). He who controls his anger has gained something great in life, self-discipline. The words of others have been so damaging that at times they can literally destroy everything we have worked for.

Fire

Fire represents going through something. I like to say it this way, if you're going through something, keep going. The only way to get stuck in something is if you stop going through something. Fire purifies things. Starting from the bottom is never easy. Starting from the bottom up will always have its purification processes, and that's a good thing. It's then that all the unpurified things come out of your life. It's better to get rid of them at the bottom than to get rid of them at the top. Being purified from the bottom up refines your significance in everything you do.

After these three things came to pass, I am sure Elijah was getting frustrated with the expectations of something big about to happen. We always set ourselves up to look for the big answers in life, but we never train ourselves to hear the gentle answers and gentle whispers in life. Whenever you want to find something of significance or build your life on the rock of significance, always be prepared to build your life in small beginnings. It is there where life will be built on a firm foundation. Zechariah tells us this, 10 Who dares despise the days of small things, since the seven eyes of the Lord that range throughout the earth will rejoice when they see the chosen capstone in the hand of Zerubbable Zech. 4:10 NIV)

A Gentle Whisper

God was not in the earthquake. God was not in the wind. God was not in the fire. Elijah found God in the gentle whisper. The earthquake, the wind, and the fire seemed like significant ways for God to get Elijah's attention while the gentle whisper seemed like the insignificant way to get Elijah's attention! We must start somewhere. We must learn how to crawl before we can ever begin to learn how to walk. A lot of times when we want to find our significance, we end up skipping the crawling process and instead jump ahead to the walking process in becoming significant. I have often wondered why God asked Elijah, "There he went into a cave and spent the night. And the word of the Lord came to him. 'What are you doing here, Elijah?'" (1 Kings 19:9 NIV)

The Crawling Process

Could it be that before we ever find ourselves walking in significance, we must first crawl in insignificance?

Think about it; when we were first learning how to crawl, we felt so insignificant. The crawling process in insignificance can represent a wide range of different things.

Disabilities: Crawling around in the insignificance of disabilities. These hit home for me with having learning disabilities and being half deaf out of my left ear. By the way, I used to be completely deaf out of my left ear. How many can relate with me in this area? I am sure there are many. It makes us feel so insignificant. To get from the crawling process of insignificance to the walking process of significance, we have to be willing to do three things.

1. Let go of feeling sorry for yourself. God made you to be you. Don't be afraid to ask for H.E.L.P.: Hinged, Evidence, Loving, People: Hinged evidence that loving people want to help you crawl in your disabilities before you can walk in your disabilities. I will encourage you to look up the ministry "A Life Without Limbs." Embrace your disabilities in the crawling process; then, that way, you will be able to embrace your disabilities in walking in your significance.

Teachable: We will always be crawling around if we are never teachable. We must relearn something to gain something. With culture changing, with society changing, with new things always coming up, we must remain teachable. It's been said that once you learn how to do something one way, it is hard in how to relearn it and do it differently.

2. Let's face it; we don't know everything, and there are always those closed off areas in our lives that we need to be teachable to learn and grow. Yet, we never open those closed off areas, then we find ourselves wondering why we can't put something together. For instance, I don't like reading instruction books on how to put stuff together, and I always end up messing up something. The life instruction manual demands that we be teachable and have the willingness to relearn. Insignificance will always leave crawling, because it is not teachable, but significance will always cause you to grow and become teachable. I believe everyone should have the quality to be teachable. Let's fling wide those closed off doors of crawling around and not being teachable and instead walk in stride to become teachable in every area of our lives.

The "What if" Mentality

If we allow ourselves to, we will begin to convince ourselves that we can't live a significant lifestyle. Has it ever happened that you wanted to do something or to accomplish something and the "what ifs" begin to drift into your mind? Instead of allowing the "what ifs" of life to change the direction of our dreams, significance, let's allow the what ifs in our minds to rechange our mentality.

3. We must know how to maneuver the thought processes of our minds. We must learn how to change life's "what ifs" in life into the right directions that point us toward the right destinations, instead of allowing the "what ifs" to guide us into wrong directions that ultimately lead us into the wrong destinations and into areas that we don't want to go. "Let this mind be in you, which was also in Christ Jesus" (Phil. 2:5 King James Version). Therefore, prepare your minds for action, be completely sober [in spirit-steadfast, self-disciplined, spiritually and morally alert], fix your hope completely on the grace [of God] that is coming to you when Jesus Christ is revealed. (1 Peter 1:13 Amplified Bible). "Let not your mind wonder or drift, let not your mind dwell on the negative what ifs in life, only let your mind dwell on the positive what ifs of life." What have the "what ifs" of life talked you out of accomplishing.

In the Middle of the Storm

In the middle of the storm is the place where you can find your greatest significance and value. If you're in a storm, it's because God trusts you in that storm. Influence the storm by self-control knowing that there is a purpose in the storm for greater significance. Responding with self-control in the middle of the storm will often propel you into the places where other people are in the middle of their own storm to let them know that they are significant.

4. "Not only so, but we also rejoice in our sufferings, because we know that suffering produces perseverance; perseverance, character; and character, hope. and hope does not put us to shame, because God's love has been poured out his love into our hearts through the Holy Spirit, who has been given to us" (Rom. 5:3–5 NIV).

Why did God make me the way that I am? Have you ever considered that? There is only one you; there is no one else like you, but, yet, we are all constantly pressed with this question, Although I can't fully answer this question, hopefully I can give you better understanding in how you were created and made the way that you are, I believe this question has stopped the movement of people journeying into their journey.

5. "Then God said let us make man in our image, in our likeness." A note on Genesis 1:26 says this, "Knowing that we are made in God's image and thus share many of his characteristics provides a solid basis for our self-worth. Knowing that we are created in his image denounces everything else." The note goes onto say human worth is not based on possessions, achievements, physical attractiveness, or public acclaim. Time out: Those key words are often the things that cause us to question in a negative way why we are the way we are. Just a side note: let's continue in what the note on Genesis 1:26 says instead and remember that because we bear God's image, because we are made in his image, we can feel positive about ourselves.

6.

Thank You to My Life Speakers

I want to dedicate these final pages to the people I call Life Speakers. I recognize and realize that their life speaking words penetrated the walls of negativity that had me bound. There are many people I could name, but there are only a few Gods has used to propel me into significance (You know who you are, and I am grateful and always encouraged by your inspiring words to me on Facebook).

37 No, in all these things we are more than *conquerors through him who loved us*. 38 For I am convinced that neither *death nor life, neither angels nor demons, neither the present nor the future, nor any powers,39 neither height nor depth, nor anything else in all creation, will be able to separate us from the love of god that is in Christ Jesus our Lord.* (Romans 8:37–39 NIV)

Conquerors: Masters

I remember the times we had together, For every mountain he brought us each over is a testament to his goodness. I recall the times of our struggles and how we were there for each other, holding each other up. You guys believed in me when I didn't have any belief in myself.

Conquerors: PB

Thanks for being a constant reminder to me that I can overcome being negative. That there is potential in me and for seeing potential in me as a father figure. Thanks for never giving up on me and always believing in me. I remember at the end of my second year when you asked me If I was ready to begin a new journey.

Conquerors: PK

I remember that you were the first father figure who instilled in me the strength and love of a father. Conquerors, you helped me overcome Goliaths in my life that first year in ways only a father could do. We shall keep swinging those sling shots to take down the Goliaths.

Past Masters

You guys brought so much healing to my life. You guys were my first glimpse of what the true meaning of family truly is to me. Every time I wanted to go back to the old negative me, you guys were always there for me, telling me that I can do it, and cheering me on as I began to share dreams. My first glimpse of significance in my life was revealed to me by you guys. I love you guys; by believing in me and being family to me, you were the key to the door that unlocked my significance.

Past PB

I remember the picture frame you handed me during the second-year retreat, and how you spoke to me as a father to speak life over myself, "I am blessed and highly favored." I also remember during second year encounter weekend, during the Coram Deo, breaking the pots into so many pieces, and then you handing me that pot that looked like it was shattered, but it was held together. I remember your words to me. I believe that was a tremendous launching point of healing for me.

Past PK

You took me in as your own son and embraced me as a father. I still remember the Summer of '04 when you told me that you loved me and believed in me. Yours were the first words of "I love you" from a father figure, and your words were the first releasing point of the past for me. I still have the e-mail from a month ago telling me that I am not obligated to hold on to the things of the past and that I am freed from the things of the past.

Future Masters

I long for the day to have a family reunion to see what God has done, to see you guys again, and one day we will. We will share the moments again. We will share the laughs again. We will cry again seeing how far we have come and grown. Thank you for being the hinge on the door of my life that swings open the doors of significance. I would be honored if you guys would join me along this journey of significance as a family. As we find out more about ourselves in God every day, let's keep swinging the rallying towel. Once masters, *always* masters!

Future PB

I will carry on speaking life into the future. Thank you, PB, for speaking that over my life and for being a reminder of that to me. There is a dream tucked away in my heart that I want to do for you in the future, and in time it will come. It's something to honor you and your leadership during those two years in my life. One day I will be able to present it to you in a Masters service way. I remember the shirt and the verse on it: Blessed are those who listens to me, watching daily at my doors, waiting at my door. (Prov. 8:34 NIV). This verse will carry me into an incredible future in the Lord.

Future PK

I also have a dream tucked away in my heart that I want to give to you in the future to honor you and your leadership in my life. In the times I have felt like quitting, I still remember your words to me, telling me that God has awesome things in store for me. Words like that from a father figure mean so much to me, and they will propel me into my incredible future in the Lord. I will be man of God that drives the devil crazy in every capacity and in every area. What the devil meant for evil; God meant it good! Thank you, PK, for being used by God to help shape and mold me into a man of God.

Significance Shaped In His Hand

O House of Israel, can I not do with you as the potter does?" declares the Lord. "Like clay in the hand of the potter, so are you in my hand O House of Israel."
—Jeremiah 18:6

You no longer need the lingering defects of the clay of insignificance, God has shaped you, molded you, and reformed you into a person of significance. Those who feel insignificant, walk with me to the potter's house to be remolded into the way he created us to be. His hands know how to shape you, to create you to walk in your significance, walk in your creativity, walk in your gifts for he has given you the tools to live a significant life and he has called you to do only what he has called you to do.

Does not the potter have the right to make out of the same lump of some pottery for a noble purpose and some for common use. Four practical ways in common use in a significant life.
—Romans 9:21

- **Give**—Find ways to give your time, your talents, your resources.

- **Love**—Find ways to love and love people as you would want to be loved.

- **Serve**—Find a place to get plugged in to help communities.

- **Accept**—Accept people for who they are as you would want to be accepted!

If you are like me and have felt insignificant so many times and have questioned why you're here, I would be honored to pray this prayer with you. Let's join hands and walked together in each of our journeys to finding out how to live a significant life and seeing ourselves as significant.

Lord, help me to lead a Life of Significance. Allow me to feel the touch of the Potter again in every area of my life. To you, Lord, I surrender all my doubts. Lord, I surrender to you all my insecurities. Lord, I surrender to you all my negative reactions toward myself and others. Lord, journey with me in this journey to significance. I need you, Lord, now more than ever before. Amen.

Endnotes

1. John Maxwell book for paraphrased quote.

2. Definition of succeed.

3. Winston Churchill Quote

4. Definition of Lifestyle

5. Definition of Surrender

6. Maxwell quote on true significance.

7. John Maxwell character quote

8. Maxwell, Peaople don't care how much you know…

9. Maxwell "Leadership is influence quote.

10. "History maker" song lyrics by Martin Smith.

11. Definition of opportunity.

12. Chapter 5, Notes from Bible verse